Congratulations! You've decided to adopt a puppy and bring a lovable, tail-wagging best friend into your life for many years to come. Find your perfect match with the help of **We're Having a Puppy!**

Discover which dogs are:
- good with children
- happy in a city apartment
- in need of plenty of exercise
- most friendly and loving
- excellent watchdogs or guard dogs
- sporting dogs
- distinctive show dogs

This fun, comprehensive guide also includes important tips on puppy training, health, nutrition, and exercise—everything you need to build a happy and healthy relationship with your new best friend.

Also from St. Martin's Paperbacks

We're Having a Kitten!

We're Having a Puppy!

From the Big Decision Through the Crucial First Year

Eric Swanson

Introduction by
Allen M. Schoen, D.V.M., M.S.

St. Martin's Paperbacks

For Marc Reeves

WE'RE HAVING A PUPPY!

Cover photograph by Noeru Takizawa/Photonica.

Library of Congress Catalog Card Number: 97-22123

ISBN: 0-312-96890-6

Printed in the United States of America

St. Martin's Press hardcover edition/November 1997
St. Martin's Paperbacks edition/March 1999

St. Martin's Paperbacks are published by St. Martin's Press, 175 Fifth Avenue, New York, NY 10010.

10 9 8 7 6 5 4 3 2 1

Table of Contents

Introduction 9

Chapter 1: Should We Have a Dog? *11*

A Brief History of Dogs and People 11

What Exactly is a Dog? 13
An Unconditional Lover • Instant Family
A Friend Who Likes to Be Where You Are
Someone to Watch Over You
A Smiling Face at the Door
Membership in the Society of Dog Owners

What Else Should We Know? 19
A Long-Term Relationship
No More Spontaneous Vacations
How Much Is That Doggy in the Window?
How Much Do You Love Your Sofa?
Canine Emotions
A Brand-New Relationship to the Outdoors

Where Do We Fit In? 27
Your Job • Travel • Children
People Who Just Can't Be Around Dogs

Is It Really a Dog We Want? 31

A Questionnaire 31

Chapter 2: Yes, We Should Have a Dog! *34*

What Kind of Owner Are You? 34

What Are You Looking For in a Dog? 36
Frisky Puppies or Responsible Adults?
Athlete or Aesthete?

Colossal or Compact? • Prince or Peasant?
Male or Female? • Choosing a Healthy Dog

Where Do Dogs Come From? 41
Homes • Breeders • Shelters • Pet Stores
Veterinarians • A Few Words About Strays

Where Can We Find Out More? 47

The Role of Instinct 49

Chapter 3: The Possible Puppy 50

Breed Categories 50
Sporting Dogs • Hounds • Working Dogs
Terriers • Toys • Nonsporting Dogs
Herd Dogs

Individual Characteristics 61
Watchdogs • Guard Dogs • Loyal Dogs
Loving Dogs • Quiet Dogs • Friendly Dogs
Intelligent Dogs • Dogs Who Like Children
Dogs Who Like Cities • Dogs with Distinction

Breed Charts 80

Chapter 4: From House to Home 96

A Dog's-Eye View 96

Divisions of Territory 97
Sleeping Areas • Gates • Doghouses
Eating Areas • To Crate or Not to Crate?

Beds, Bowls, and Beyond 101
Collars and Leashes • Dog Beds • Bowls
Toys • Grooming Tools • Unmentionables

Hazards of Occupancy 106
Windows • Hot Stuff • Household Toxins

Chocolate • Plants • Cords and Strings
Sharp Things and Foreign Objects • Stairs

The Great Outdoors 110
The Blessing of Restraint • Wandering • Fences

Summary 114

Chapter 5: The Blessed Event 115

The Journey Home 116

Home at Last 117
One Room at a Time
If You're Adopting a Puppy
If You're Adopting an Older Dog
Other Dogs in the Household
Dogs and Other Animals

The First Month 126
Licensing • First Visit to the Vet
Housebreaking • Paper-Training • Schedules
Walking • Feeding • Diet

Chapter 6: Living Together 136

Training 137
Trust • Tools • Voice • Body Language
Rewards • Reprimands • Consistency
What Every Dog Should Know
Professional Options

Problem Behaviors 148
Soiling • Destructiveness • Aggression

Travel 151
Taking Your Dog with You • Traveling by Car
Public Transportation
Leaving Your Dog Home • Boarding • Moving

Grooming 157
General Procedures • Shorthairs • Longhairs
Dense Coats • Wiry, Curly, or Unusual Coats
Nail Trimming • Bathing

Breeding 163
Pedigree Breeding • Neutering

Health Care 165
Battling the Elements • Vaccinations
Infectious Diseases • Noninfectious Complaints
Internal Parasites • External Parasites
Communicable Diseases
Administering Medication • Emergency Care
Transporting Ill or Injured Dogs

In Sum 180

Chapter 7: Last Words 182

Special Needs of Older Dogs 183
Diet • Exercise • Skin and Coat
Eyes • Age-Related Illnesses

Death 186

Appendices 187

Appendix A: Registries and Publications 187

Appendix B: Pet Insurance 188

Appendix C: Toxins 189

Introduction

The human/animal bond holds great fascination for me. As a holistic veterinarian, I have witnessed firsthand the profound spiritual bond that exists between people and their beloved pets. But I have also seen the disillusionment of that relationship when unrealistic expectations or half-hearted commitments were made. These animals often end up in the hands of shelters, abandoned or euthanized.

We're Having a Puppy! is an excellent guide to the vital issues that should be considered *prior* to adopting a pet. The aim is not to discourage pet ownership, but to encourage a thoughtful decision, thereby increasing the chances of a happy union. Realistic expectations and a firm commitment are the first steps to a healthy marriage.

If you decide to take the plunge, *We're Having a Puppy!* will support you on your journey with valuable insights along the way. It will help you find a dog that's right for you, create an ideal environment that nurtures your new bond, and support you through the first crucial year. This is truly a holistic approach.

As a veterinarian, author, and animal lover, I am happy to recommend this book to all who consider sharing their life with a furry companion. Go forth, contemplate, and if it feels right, enjoy!

Allen M. Schoen, D.V.M., M.S.
Author, *Love, Miracles, and Animal Healing*

Chapter 1

Should We Have a Dog?

If you're wondering whether or not to get a dog, you're not alone. Kings and commoners alike have contemplated the same question for thousands of years. Of course, nobody's ever asked a dog whether he wants to have a person, but it's fair to say the attraction between the two species runs deep. Dogs and people just seem to fit together—like words and music, mom and apple pie, Bonnie and Clyde.

Maybe you've acquired a dog already, and you're wondering what to do now. In all likelihood, he's looking up at you from the floor as you read this, waiting for some sign of approval—a pat on the head or a kind word, something to let him know the bond between you is alive and well. If you look in his eyes right now, you'll see something you don't find elsewhere: soul. Unlike most other animals (humans included), dogs can't hide their soul. This probably accounts for a large part of their appeal. At the end of the day, it's a comfort to spend time with someone whose emotions don't need second-guessing.

A BRIEF HISTORY OF DOGS AND PEOPLE

No one can say for sure how dogs came to be the first domesticated animals, but most seem to think it happened around twenty-five thousand years ago. Even the nicer sort of people lived in caves at the time, and though a fair amount of food did grow on trees, the preferred sustenance of Cro-Magnon man was meat—which didn't usually lie about begging to be eaten. Meat had to be hunted, and it's a good guess that people hunted in groups: You'd more likely come home in one piece that way, instead of winding up in something else's stomach.

The wild ancestors of modern dogs seem to have organized themselves pretty much along the same lines. The domestic dog, *Canis familiaris*, is thought to be a direct descendant of a small subspecies of wolf, *Canis lupus pallipes* (white-footed wolf), which originated in the Middle East. Then as now, wolves lived together in caves, probably for the same reasons as early man. Caves are warm, protected from the less hospitable elements, and fairly easy to defend. More importantly, wolves live and hunt in packs. There's far less scheming or jockeying for position to be seen in canine society than among humans. Canines very sensibly follow the lead of the strongest and wisest member of the pack.

It's possible that *Canine lupus* entered the precincts of early cave dwellers as a prospective meal, narrowly avoiding this unpleasant fate by demonstrating the type of usefulness for which their descendants are known today. Perhaps deliberately misconstruing the point of being fattened for the fire, he came to see his captors as a species of stronger, wiser wolf, and instinctively offered the same services he'd perform for his own kind: defending the lair, barking at intruders, and warning off other wolves by marking the territory with urine and feces.

Or perhaps a pack of wolves resided near a human settlement, and lived off scraps of meat and bone left over after a hearty Cro-Magnon meal. Understandably desiring to protect a territory that offered such relatively easy pickings, they would have kept other packs or predators away, and may have even followed their human neighbors from camp to camp. In time, the two groups— humans and wolves—may have grown accustomed to one another, and learned to mingle in a friendly fashion.

Regardless of the manner in which wolves and humans began their happy association, the advantages of joining forces in the rough game of survival became apparent soon enough. In return for warmth, companionship, and regular meals, *Canis lupus* offered his keen instincts and abilities both for hunting and protecting the settlement. Eventually, through a combined process of selective breeding and spontaneous mutation, *Canis familiaris* evolved into a family that includes more than four hundred different breeds. Some bloodlines are quite venerable, indeed: the loyal Samoyed hunted reindeer alongside Asiatic nomads more than seven thousand years ago, while the regal Saluki were revered by ancient Sumerians thousands of years before their upstart neighbors on the Nile built the first pyramid.

Archeological discoveries have shown that dogs played a significant role in early cultures throughout Europe and the Far East. Captain Cook observed dogs happily serving the inhabitants of the remote islands of the Pacific, while the dingo has inhabited Australia for centuries. Probably the oldest *Canis familiaris* skeleton yet found—believed to be more than ten thousand years old—was unearthed recently in Idaho. Exactly how dogs managed to travel from the Middle East to such far-flung regions remains a mystery, but it is clear they have enjoyed a special place in human society long before cats, cows, and canaries.

This high regard for *Canis familiaris* has been recorded in art and literature through the ages. Perhaps one of the best-known tales of canine loyalty can be found toward the end of Homer's *Odyssey*—when the hero's dog, after waiting twenty years for his master to return, summons his last bit of vital energy to wag his tail. Painters and sculptors, meanwhile, have for eons busied themselves representing the canine form. Ancient Persians carved images of greyhound-like dogs on their rich tombs. The Egyptians of four thousand years ago decorated their walls with images of lean, elegant Pharaoh hounds. European masters such as Titian, Gainsborough, and Van Dyke included dogs in family portraits and pastoral scenes, much as contemporary family albums include at least one engaging photo of little Rover or Angélique.

WHAT EXACTLY IS A DOG?

Since before the dawn of recorded history, dogs have served humanity as workers, playmates, and boon companions. They have watched over children, driven rats from home and hearth, protected the widow, the orphan, and the lonely hermit, and defended the farmer's livestock from poachers of both the animal and human variety. Civilizations have crumbled, institutions have fallen away, the humble oxcart has been replaced by the jumbo jet—yet the essential bond between human and canine has remained virtually unchanged. Modern dogs patrol the home front and nip the heels of recalcitrant sheep; they sniff out drugs and explosives; they rescue toddlers, the ill, and the elderly from dangerous situations.

Cynics may deride such behavior as an example of foolish consistency, or a devastating failure of imagination. Dogs rarely believe the worst about themselves, however, and their delight in people seldom wanes. The basic canine nature may be summed up as the hope of love returned in equal measure to love offered.

No doubt such loyalty is grounded in a dog's natural inclination to obey the leader of the pack. Yet this capacity to extend allegiance to another species touches on the miraculous, and deserves to be cherished.

Character varies with each breed of dog, of course, as well as among individuals within a particular breed. Still, most dogs share a number of similar traits regardless of bloodline or individual history. These include:

- Devotion
- Trust
- Rapport
- Concern
- Friendliness
- Charisma

Though initially the list of canine qualities may read like the preamble of a Boy Scout meeting, dogs are by no means simple creatures. Their inner workings are as finely calibrated as any of nature's more ingenious creations. Perhaps the best way to appreciate this fact is to examine each characteristic in more detail.

An Unconditional Lover

Like much of canine prehistory, the identity of the person who first dubbed the dog "man's best friend" is shrouded in the mists of time. Few, however, can dispute the absolute fitness of the title. What other creature will listen raptly to the same tall tale fifty times over and never betray a hint of boredom, or lend a perpetually sympathetic—if somewhat floppy—ear to the same complaints over money, the boss, the neighbors, or the in-laws? Who will greet you with the same pristine joy each morning, no matter how your breath smells or which way your hair is sitting? To whom does it honestly not matter what you're wearing when you go out in public together?

Dogs do not judge by appearances. In fact, where their owners are concerned, they do not judge at all. This is perhaps the single most attractive quality dogs have to offer, a type of enlightened vision of the soul. When your dog looks at you, she sees you— not your job, not your taste in art, and certainly not your breeding potential. Nor does she see your defects of character, the secret names you call yourself to prove your frailty. She sees only your glory, your fully realized potential. People have striven for countless generations to achieve the same compassionate outlook upon their fellows. To dogs, it just comes naturally.

A brief comparison with other types of pets may illustrate this point more clearly. Cats, for example, possess extremely refined emotions, yet their entire evolutionary development has been geared toward solitary survival; they will give pleasure where pleasure is given—they have been known to caress and even lick their prey (after it's dead)—but their primary drive remains one of self-satisfaction. Rodents, meanwhile, may look sweet, but they're more apt to bite or scurry down a hole than to rest their wee heads in your lap while you watch the news. And with all due respect to marine life, one rarely hears "cold as a fish" offered as a compliment.

Unconditional love can be a bit harrowing at first for those unaccustomed to its responsibilities and rewards. Even well-adjusted persons may find it uncomfortable to be seen so nakedly, and desired so openly. The human heart is a curious thing, full of secret passages and forbidden entries. Don't be surprised, therefore, if you feel a tingle of resistance to your dog's attempts to occupy the entire organ. It's only natural, and won't offend Sadie in the least. Slowly but surely, she'll find a way to unlock the hidden doors and show you treasures in yourself you never knew existed. This may be the most harrowing day of all. When you realize you love your dog as deeply as she loves you, you'll understand the real value of an open heart, and what it will mean to lose it.

Instant Family

Popular psychology has fostered an understanding that individuals do not choose the families into which they are born. This has not always been the prevailing opinion, however, and even now certain esoteric writers challenge this view. While the issue is not likely to be resolved any time soon, most people agree that family members tend to adapt to one another. In spite of any manifest or subtle dysfunction, a certain trust develops in every family. It may consist of knowing that one's elder brother will always attempt to bring about one's demise, or that one's mother will always exhibit a degree of cantankerousness in the grocery store. Still, family can be counted on to be exactly as they are, and to perceive us exactly as they always have.

Dogs rarely choose their owners; and no matter how much thought you give to selecting your pet, until the two of you have lived together a while, an element of uncertainty necessarily colors your relationship. Yet in very short order, the same type of intimacy develops between dog and owner as between sister and brother, or parent and child. Dogs adapt to their owners with very little complaint, and in this atmosphere of acceptance, most owners find it easy to relate to their pets with the same degree of familiarity. The comfort that grows out of this type of relationship transcends exchanging solace in times of trouble, or sharing pleasurable activities such as hiking, swimming, or antagonizing squirrels. It's a rock-solid knowing that you can count on each other to be the way you are.

At times, you'll be astonished by the empathy that flows from your dog to you. When you're blue, he may try to lighten your load by putting on a show or encouraging you to play a hearty game of fetch; when you're happy, he'll celebrate right alongside you. The way he looks at you when you're confused, licks your face when you're upset, or huddles close to keep you warm when you're ill, may convince you he is endowed with human understanding. It's tempting to think of your dog as a person trapped inside a fur coat.

More accurately, though, he's a wolf that has kindly consented to conform to human habits. Like other wild creatures, wolves possess a type of sensitivity that has to some extent been bred out of humans. Changes in posture, body rhythm, intonation, and personal scent are significant to dogs in ways mankind no longer notices. More specifically, dogs instinctively attune themselves to their leaders' slightest behavioral suggestions, because survival in the wild depends on rapid and appropriate group response. Because you have given him a home, food, affection, and warmth, your dog quite naturally offers you the gift of his extraordinary sensitivity.

Of course, no matter how well you and your dog understand each other, unpleasant surprises will occur from time to time. You may come home from a long day at the office and find the living room sofa reduced to a shapeless mass of chewed foam rubber. Or perhaps, after you've just received your forty-ninth rejection of your latest novel, your dog may have to bear an angry outburst. But the bond between you can sustain such blows. Rex's honest remorse will encourage you to forgive him for the sofa, and your tantrum won't alter his excellent opinion of you. Though tempests threaten, love remains.

Family life requires commitment, however. Harmony depends on each member recognizing that no one in the household has yet attained a godlike self-sufficiency. While most family roles have shifted somewhat from the traditional model in recent years, the essential relation between dog and master has remained fairly constant. Just as you depend on Rover to defend your home, warn against intruders, or amuse Aunt Sally with his latest trick, so he relies on you to fulfill needs he can't supply himself. The precise nature of your responsibilities will be explored later in this chapter. For now, it's enough to know that intimacy—no matter how immediate or genuine—is never a free ride.

A Friend Who Likes to Be Where You Are

It is not uncommon for a pall of dissatisfaction to descend on even the most congenial relationship, once the novelty of being together has worn off. Although this tends to occur more generally when both partners belong to the same species, misfortunes of this sort are not unknown among members of different classes of the animal kingdom. One morning, your cat may simply cease to be amused; or you may remove the cover from Polly's cage and discover, to your chagrin, that your witty, engaging parrot is just another crabby bird hooked on crackers.

Dog owners are less likely to experience the traumas associated with familiarity. Something genuinely profound begins to take shape from the outset, so subtly it may take a while to notice. The day will come, however, when you realize that your dog does not simply love and respect you. She has taken refuge in you: To her, you are home. Circumstances may force you from your dream house to a cardboard box (or vice versa); you may decide to relinquish the questionable blessings of stability and become a merry wanderer of the road; you could, like the Desert Fathers, take up residence atop a pillar in the sands of Egypt. Regardless of the path you choose, your dog will follow.

Many dogs appear to enjoy a change of scene now and again. At least, confronting new territory doesn't seem to provoke the same degree of anxiety seen in other types of pets. Dogs therefore make excellent traveling companions, happily vacationing with their owners in all corners of the world where they are welcome. Naturally, taking a pet along for even a weekend junket involves special preparations, which will be examined in Chapter Six. So long as you're within sniffing range, however, dogs are equally content to sit at home watching reruns, or dozing by the pool. Or simply taking a Sunday drive. Whatever your idea of a good time is, it's bound to be Bowser's as well.

Someone to Watch Over You

As suggested earlier, security may have been one of the prime factors behind early man's decision to domesticate dogs rather than eat them. Yet even in our modern age, dogs still offer their owners an extra measure of protection. Armed with an exceptionally keen sense of hearing and smell, dogs can detect the approach of potential intruders at a greater distance than many sophisticated security systems. Although the suspected interloper may just as likely turn out to be the paperboy as a midnight thief, a dog will sound a rather noisy alarm, regardless. However, since a dog can't be accidentally turned off or deliberately disconnected, even indiscriminate barking has its advantages. Meanwhile, most people find it more satisfying to curl up next to a dog than an electronic eye.

Dogs have also been known to alert people to other threatening situations, such as fires or medical emergencies. Literature abounds with examples of canine heroics, which range from leading lost children home, to rescuing alpine climbers, to fighting off bears, wolves, and rattlesnakes while distraught picnickers run for cover. Yet even those who venture into no more hazardous territory than their quiet suburban street will doubtless feel more secure at night with a dog by their side, since the slightest whiff of danger will trigger a canine's defensive response.

A Smiling Face at the Door

Especially after a long, hard day, it's extremely pleasant to be greeted by someone who adores you. No matter how low your opinion of yourself has sunk, no matter what you've accomplished or failed to accomplish, no matter how late you are for dinner, your dog can't wait to let you know how wonderful you really are. Even if his bladder is full to bursting, you're still wonderful. And of course, after you've gone for that quick but vitally necessary walk, you're even more terrific still: You may be grumpy, tired, cold, or soggy, but chances are, you'll find it hard to hang on to a bitter mood with so much positive feeling focused on you.

Among animate creatures, dogs alone seem endowed with seemingly relentless good humor. A person would have to deliberately abuse a dog over a long period in order to undermine his natural buoyancy. Some people do, of course—believing the only way to train a dog is to break his spirit. They're quite wrong; the only possible result of overtly harsh training is a tense, irritable, and possibly aggressive animal. Unfortunately, this particular training myth retains a strong hold on the popular imagination. Proper training methods will be discussed in Chapters Five and Six.

Membership in the Society of Dog Owners

You've seen them on the street and in the park. They huddle together on beaches, at barbecues, and picnics; perhaps you've even glimpsed them in airports or the parking lot of your local supermarket. They always have something to talk about—a dialogue both animated and arcane, from which you may have felt, at times, excluded. From afar, it may appear that dog owners are blessed with social skills that the dogless can never hope to attain.

They aren't, of course; it's simply that dogs afford excellent openings for conversation. They can be praised, scolded, and analyzed in ways a spouse, a child, or a friend may not. While the average husband, for example, may take umbrage if a stranger happens to scratch his wife's head and comment on the beauty of her tail, chances are a dog owner will accept such compliments more graciously. Some may find the sudden flood of attention a bit wearying, especially when time or temper does not suit social intercourse. Fortunately, even when they are the object of admiration, most dogs don't stand still very long. There's always something new to explore, a grand adventure around the corner just waiting to be discovered. So even a relatively shy owner has a ready excuse to move on should the kindness of strangers prove trying.

WHAT ELSE SHOULD WE KNOW?

Even a modest amount of worldly experience can illuminate the connection between happiness and responsibility. When it comes to dogs, however, people tend to forget the lessons they've learned in life. They see only the good times they can share with their pet, paying scant heed to the obligations that may attend ownership. If you're thinking of having a dog, you ought to consider the following factors before making up your mind:

- Canine longevity
- Your personal freedom
- Expenses
- Your attachment to possessions
- Temperamental differences
- Your attitude toward the great outdoors

People who aren't prepared to meet a dog's physical and emotional needs should consider another type of pet. Animal shelters teem with dogs who have been abandoned by owners citing various excuses, from the birth of a new baby, to allergic spouses, to relocation overseas. While a small percentage of sorry tales may be true, the vast majority are utter falsehoods. It is far more likely that these owners hadn't considered the responsibilities of daily care, or had chosen a dog without taking their particular circumstances or the dog's temperament and history into account.

Of course, allergies, relocation, and behavioral problems can raise serious difficulties for dog owners. They are not, however, an excuse for simply dropping a dog in the woods or along the side of a road. Dogs are not necessarily wise in the ways of traffic; neither can they subsist for long in wet or freezing weather, or on a diet of garbage. Abandoned dogs tend to suffer cruelly.

Should you encounter a stray dog, the kindest thing to do is to bring him to a shelter. He may be lost, and his heartsick owners may be looking for him. If you're totally smitten with him, of course, you can make adoption arrangements with the shelter; if he isn't claimed after an agreed-upon time period, you can take him home with you. Naturally, should you decide to keep him, you must bring him to a veterinarian for a thorough examination.

A Long-Term Relationship

Whether or not the attention span of the average person has diminished significantly in response to the wealth of stimuli available today is a matter of some debate. Perhaps the single greatest obstacle to verifying this hypothesis lies in the difficulty of locating persons whose characters were formed two or three centuries prior to our own. If any do still walk the earth, they have remained singularly reticent. Nevertheless, in recent years a large number of commentators have observed that men and women of the modern age exhibit a conspicuous taste for immediate gratification. They want what they want without delay; and when they have satisfied a whim, they divest themselves of all traces of their former preoccupation with equal haste. Upon such fickle attitudes many rewarding legal practices have been built.

Relatively few repercussions ensue when the coveted object is inanimate. A dog, however, is fully conscious, enormously sensitive, and almost entirely dependent upon his owners for affection, sustenance, grooming, and excretory activities. Moreover, this dependence can last a very long time. While a splendid animal such as a Great Dane or Saint Bernard may go the way of all flesh in a matter of eight or ten human years, smaller breeds, such as poodles or toys, quite often see a ripe old age of twelve to fifteen years. In the bluntest possible terms, this means twelve to fifteen years or more of stocking kibbles and canned food, venturing out into rain, snow, and dark of night to visit the fire hydrant, choosing residences and planning vacations where dogs are welcome, and finding partners who share an enthusiasm for canines.

Of course, if you're emotionally and financially prepared to meet these obligations, you'll enjoy many of the same benefits you'd derive from other sorts of committed relationships. The blessing of familiarity and the comfort of growing old with someone who loves you are not to be discounted. At the same time, naturally, you'll probably deal with many of the same frustrations and compromises that beset long-term partners. Dogs, like spouses, seem particularly adept at tuning out rational argument; raising your voice isn't going to make them hear any better.

No More Spontaneous Vacations

In many ways, owning a dog is like having a child: Your days of freedom aren't necessarily over, but you'll have to redefine the term. You can, for example, leave a dog home for several hours while you go to work, do some shopping, or enjoy a romantic evening of wine and song. Like Cinderella, though, you'll have to keep an eye on the clock. Eight or ten hours after his last walk, Prince will start fidgeting near the front door due to an urgent need to relieve his swollen bladder. And if you're too late serving dinner, he may already have taken a few bites out of your glass slippers.

Accordingly, your normal schedule will have to undergo some adjustment. Maybe you're accustomed to arriving home after work and taking a shower, or watching the news, or returning phone calls. Before you fall into your routine, though, Fifi has to take care of a bit of important business. Since she's been cooped up inside all day, a quick trip down to the corner and back probably won't satisfy her appetite for exercise. If you work at home, you'll probably find that she gets bored with her toys after a while, and yearns for the kind of stimulation only you can give. And if you're normally an early riser, chances are slim you'll get to enjoy an occasional late morning. Unless you keep her out of the room, your darling girl will strike up a conversation at just about the time the alarm clock usually sounds.

Long absences from home require a bit of forethought. Not only must you provide for your dog's physical needs, you'll also need to consider her emotional well-being. Dogs are social animals (much more so than your average debutante). Deprived of companionship for too long, they can become depressed, anxious, destructive, and possibly ill. If you know you're going to be away from home for a while, arrange for a friend, relative, neighbor—or even a professional dog-walker—to look after your dog. Ideally, Fifi should be on friendly terms with her temporary caretaker. You'll at least have to introduce the two, so she doesn't mistake her sitter for a prowler.

Of course, you may wish to take her with you. Many hotels, motels, and other types of lodging welcome well-behaved pets. You may have to search a bit for the right place, and the cost may be a little higher than normal, but the benefits usually outweigh the disadvantages. You won't have to worry whether Fifi is receiving all the care and attention she needs, you'll enjoy all the security you're accustomed to at home, and you won't want for companionship in a strange place.

Finally, canine emergencies may require you to rearrange your priorities on occasion. Such situations may be relatively minor (i.e., running out of kibbles) or critical (e.g, illness or accidents). While you might be able to avoid an early morning run to the grocery store by serving up dinner leftovers, more serious situations call for immediate action. You may feel silly canceling a golf game or taking time off from work because your dog is sick, but dogs don't fake illness or pretend to be hit by a car just to get attention. Unusual symptoms, such as chronic vomiting or diarrhea, fever, coughing, and difficulty urinating or defecating, demand prompt veterinary attention.

How Much Is That Doggy in the Window?

The price of adoption is merely the first dog-related expense you need to consider; it is also, over time, a comparatively minor outlay. Before deciding to acquire a dog, you must therefore determine whether you can realistically afford to keep him. Typical expenditures include:

Food. Although domesticated dogs no longer hunt for their supper, their dietary requirements remain the same as for their predatory ancestors. Wild canines typically eat not only the muscles and organs of their prey, but also the bones and whatever undigested food remains in the stomach and intestines of the unfortunate victim. In this way, they satisfy their need for protein, minerals, vitamins, and an odd assortment of glandular secretions. In order to give your dog a sufficiently wholesome diet, you'll either have to purchase commercially prepared food, or prepare a meal that includes low-fat meat, cereal or rice, bonemeal or calcium supplements, and vegetables. A steady diet of table scraps will not supply all the nutrients your dog needs.

Caretaking. If you're going to be away from home for more than ten hours a day, you'll need to make arrangements for someone to feed, water, and walk your dog. Many people who are away from home all day arrange for someone to walk their dog at least once a day. If you're going to be away overnight or longer, you must either arrange for someone to look in on him, or board him at a kennel.

Toys. For dogs, toys do not represent merely a gratuitous indulgence. Dogs need to chew, not only to maintain jaw muscle tone, but also to keep their teeth clean and strong. Chew toys will be destroyed regularly with use, but this does not mean you can sacrifice quality. Cheap plastic toys can be swallowed in the course of normal shredding, and the synthetic materials may become lodged in your dog's digestive tract, or otherwise lead to illness. Similarly, avoid articles made of soft or splintery wood. To satisfy your dog's chewing habit safely, regularly offer toys made of solid rubber or rawhide.

License Fees. An unlicensed lost or stray dog can be taken to the pound and executed. To avoid tragic misunderstandings of this sort, it is vital to pay for a license; in return, you will receive a metal tag that your dog must wear around his collar at all times. Typically, such tags include a dog's name and his owner's contact information. License fees, terms, and conditions vary from state to state, and country to country. For information pertaining to your particular locale, contact your local humane society or shelter. In fact, if you acquire your dog from a pound or shelter, you will not be able to leave the premises without obtaining a license.

Liability Insurance. Dogs can get into trouble from time to time. They can destroy a neighbor's shrubbery, chew something that doesn't belong to them, or, worst of all, attack a person or another dog. For people who own property, liability for damage may be covered in the general policy (even so, it's good to review the policy with your broker). If you're not covered, you should invest in liability insurance before you have to pay for damage to Farmer MacGregor's garden.

Handling Equipment. Most cities require that dogs be walked on a leash. Naturally, this means you will also have to purchase a collar or harness to which the leash must be attached. In addition, many owners purchase special choke chains or collars for training purposes. Even if your city does not legally bind you to leash your dog, it's wise to do so, as you will be able to control his behavior more closely when you venture together into the outside world. Don't tempt fate by supposing that he'll respond at all times to verbal commands. His wild instincts may prove too powerful when confronted by the opportunity to chase a squirrel or attack a strange dog; and if, in his exuberance, he inflicts damage on another person or another's property, or if he dashes in front of a car, it will be too late to curse your arrogance.

Carriers, Crates, and Other Accommodations. If you intend to travel with your dog, you will need a carrier that conforms to the specifications of the airline, bus line, or other public conveyance you may use during the course of your trip. Often, these carriers serve double duty as sleeping accommodations for indoor dogs. Some owners—and their dogs—prefer more attractive and comfortable arrangements, such as a large firm pillow or dog bed. As den animals, however, many dogs prefer the security of a crate or cage, to which they can retire when necessary. The issue of "crating" a dog has inspired some controversy and will be examined more closely in Chapter Four.

Medical expenses. Common medical expenses include yearly checkups, immunizations and booster shots, and neutering or spaying. These will be discussed more thoroughly in Chapter Six. However, bear in mind that immunization, booster shots, and tests for common canine diseases are absolutely essential—not only for your dog's well-being, but for that of the people around her. Dogs can carry viruses, fungi, and other unpleasant parasites that may be hazardous to human health. Meanwhile, depending on the type of treatment involved, medical costs can rise dramatically if your dog is injured or develops a serious illness. Fortunately, pet insurance is now available from several sources. Your veterinarian, local animal shelter, or local animal hospital should be able to advise you about insurance carriers. A more complete discussion of insurance can be found in Appendix B.

How Much Do You Love Your Sofa?

People develop attachments to worldly goods to a degree most dogs do not. To a dog, a thing is useful only insofar as it may be chewed, shredded, or chased, while surfaces are for sleeping or bowel relief. Accordingly, housebreaking is probably the most distressing ritual for the new owner of a puppy. Few people consider stepping into a puddle of puppy urine a grand adventure; on the other hand, it is rarely convenient to line every floor and surface of the home with newspaper.

Unfortunately, dogs that have not been housebroken have no idea what the fuss is all about, until persistent training has fixed in their minds the relationship between the need to relieve themselves and humbly requesting access to the outside world. Constant vigilance on your part is required until the association has been indelibly etched; and when you are not available, puppy will need to be confined to his crate or a newspaper-lined room.

Only slightly less grisly than finding your home transformed into a canine comfort station is the discovery of tooth and claw marks in your shoes, sofa, handbag, or other unlikely objects. Teething puppies chew just about anything. Some dogs are just born chewers, however, and both puppies and older dogs have been known to ruin household goods wantonly when overwhelmed by a fear of abandonment or the stress of adapting to new surroundings. As with housebreaking, you'll need to keep a watchful eye out for behavior of this sort, and put a stop to it as soon as it is observed. Otherwise, Dasher will come to believe that gnawing armchair cushions and shredding tea cozies is occasionally acceptable.

Canine Emotions

For the most part, dogs have fairly predictable emotional habits. Around their owners, they radiate love and joy. When strangers call, they may snap into a protective mode. If beset by stress or fear, they can make hash of the nearest dried flower arrangement. In the early stages of training, you'll likely find that your dog has a stubborn streak; getting her to sit, heel, or lie down may require certain physical manipulations on your part, until she understands the seriousness of your intent. Meanwhile, the outside world, strange surroundings, and other people present such a fascinating array of odors and other stimuli, you will probably need to command your dog's attention repeatedly.

Occasions may arise when you simply don't feel up to a long walk or a drawn-out game of fetch. In such cases, some type of compromise will have to be worked out. Dogs are by nature energetic creatures, and if deprived of constructive outlets for their vitality, they will occupy themselves with less respectable exertions. A moderately brisk or lengthy walk, or a few rounds of fetch the knucklebone is infinitely preferable to a clandestine round of dissect the duvet.

Certain temperamental problems may also jeopardize harmonious relations. Inconsistent or incomplete early training may render a dog permanently incapable of grasping simple household rules. Dogs abused by previous owners often develop a surly, jealous, or wrathful streak, which even the most tender attention cannot completely eradicate. Similarly, frightening experiences can undermine a dog's confidence for days, months, or even years. And because their feelings run deep, grief over the loss of a human or animal companion may never be entirely healed. In all such cases, you will need to exert special care to provide a nurturing, mutually supportive environment.

A Brand-New Relationship to the Outdoors

The perceptive reader will no doubt have gathered by now that, unlike almost any other type of domestic pet, dogs need to spend a fair amount of time outside. The precise amount depends on the size and physical aptitude of the dog in question. Large, active types, such as greyhounds or borzois, require frequent bouts of vigorous exercise. Smaller breeds, such as papillons or shih tzus, still require daily doses of fresh air and exercise, but are not usually excited by the prospect of jogging or keeping pace with a bicycle.

In any case, dogs do not make suitable pets for the agoraphobic or for those who fundamentally detest inclement weather. Morning and evening, regardless of temperature or humidity, a dog simply must venture beyond the front door, if for no other purpose than to relieve himself. A wise owner never makes an exception for a housebroken dog, for a single omission is the devil's doorway.

A final note about outdoor excursions is appropriate at this juncture. The wide world does not belong exclusively to you and your dog. In practical terms, this means you absolutely must direct your pet toward an untrammeled spot for the relief of urinary discomfort and remove any solid waste your dog deposits if there is even the remotest chance another person will pass through the area. Few things in life can damage friendly relations between people as readily as a misadventure involving canine excretions.

WHERE DO WE FIT IN?

People tend to be more complicated than dogs, and somewhat less forthright. Before opening your life to an animal who will, after all, depend on you for many things, it's wise to take a long, hard look at your current commitments and personal habits. Wherever possible, avoid self-flattery. Since no handbook can completely prepare prospective owners for the surprise of dealing daily with a living, breathing animal, a firm grasp of your own limitations will make the initial period of adjustment much easier to bear.

Your Job

Dogs do not generally make ideal companions for extremely busy people. They must be walked two or three times a day, and contact with the outside world makes at least weekly grooming essential. It is pointless, moreover, to leave a bowl of food out all day in hopes that Max will take a nibble now and then when hunger calls. Instinct usually compels a dog to bolt down everything set before him, which means he'll spend the rest of the day wandering the apartment, fretting over when the next meal will be served.

If more than one person shares your household, chances are your dog's physical needs will be properly attended to. He will probably also receive the social interaction on which his emotional well-being depends. If you live alone, however, a string of lonely days with no one to play with may cause undue stress. Though some breeds can tolerate solitude more graciously than others, even a relatively serene dog may greet a long-absent owner rather more rambunctiously than is really preferred—to say nothing of the destructive behavior desperation may drive him to adopt.

If you work long hours, you'll have to compensate for your absence by giving your dog a good deal of concentrated attention during your waking hours at home. Not everyone is capable of doing this after a hectic day, although many people find that a long walk outdoors or a hearty wrestling match erodes the stress that accumulates after a long day of dealing with odious human companions. It may be worth your while, however, to adopt more than one dog, so they can keep each other company while away.

Travel

If travel is a regular part of your professional duties, you must make arrangements for someone to walk, feed, and amuse your dog three times a day while you're out of town. Even so, prolonged or frequent absences on your part will cause her a great deal of stress. She probably won't spend hours on the phone complaining to her mother, or leave you a note saying she's gone to Vermont for a week to think things over—but she'll feel your rejection keenly. A loving heart is easily broken. You might make amends by occasionally taking her with you.

Traveling together is not always practical, of course; and if you can't arrange for someone to stay or play with your dog, you'll need to board her. The best possible setting would be the home of someone who likes dogs, and perhaps is already acquainted with yours. Failing this, you'll need to investigate a kennel. While not the most attractive solution, from a canine perspective, kennels are rarely Dickensian horror chambers; a large proportion of them are well maintained, by people who adore dogs. Still, being locked in a cage surrounded by a group of yapping, barking strangers may, understandably, be interpreted as a prison sentence. In Chapter Six, we'll look more closely at the issues involved in traveling with your dog and boarding her.

Children

Generally speaking, dogs and children seem to have been designed for each other. Their energy levels are just about evenly matched, as is the delight both take in performing repetitive activities that tend to bore or exhaust an adult.

It's crucial to note, however, that not all breeds exhibit an affinity for children. Some feel threatened by a child's high spirits, and will hold themselves a bit aloof, while others actively dislike children altogether. Dogs that have been abused, or that have suffered unpleasant experiences around children, may respond either nervously or aggressively. The question of compatibility will be examined more closely in Chapter Three.

Around newborns, dogs don't usually exhibit the same degree of jealousy as other types of pets. As long as you're around the house, Wilbur probably won't suffer pangs of rejection—though you may find he'll respond to whatever attention you give him with a bit more enthusiasm than usual. It's vital, however, to allow him to spend some supervised time around the new arrival. Otherwise, he may conclude that this isolated creature is not a true member of the pack. Let him sniff the child while you talk to him quietly, but restrain him from licking or nipping; babies are simply not old enough to play, even gently. Some dogs respond adversely to the sound of crying. Perhaps they misinterpret the sound as a challenge or warning; perhaps they simply can't tolerate the noise or become confused by it. To be on the safe side, keep your dog away from infants in distress.

Once your dog understands that baby is part of the pack, he'll probably endeavor to protect this weakest member from any sort of threat. Unfortunately, adoring grandparents and overweening great-aunts tend to be absorbed in this category rather easily. It is well to advise visitors not to swoop down on the infant until your dog has had a chance to see that baby enjoys being handled by individuals outside the family group.

The situation changes somewhat when baby begins to waddle about and investigate the world around him. At this point, your dog may need protection. Young children often use excessive force when exploring their surroundings, and should therefore be restrained from any attempt to ingest or otherwise intrude too violently upon their four-footed companions. Grabbing, poking, and biting may injure your dog, or, worse, cause him to retaliate.

Until children are old enough to understand the consequences of their actions—usually between the ages of five and twenty-five—all interactions should be carefully supervised.

Finally, many handbooks and even a few dog owners suggest that children can be taught to share the responsibilities of caring for a dog; some even go so far as to insinuate that children will enjoy such tasks as walking, feeding, and grooming. One must wonder what sort of children are imagined in these scenarios. To be sure, a passion for duty may inspire some children, but experience has shown this to be the exception rather than the rule. A dog is the responsibility of the person who acquired him, and one must never expect one's spouse, siblings, roommates, or children to share the burden with any degree of willingness.

People Who Just Can't Be Around Dogs

Allergies to dog hair are less common than other types of pet-related allergies, but some people do experience mild or severe reactions. It is, unfortunately, a myth that breeds that shed only a small amount or not at all are less likely to provoke an allergic response. Allergies are caused by proteins in the animals' saliva that are released during grooming. These proteins become airborne and quickly penetrate an entire living space. It's possible that certain people can tolerate the chemicals secreted by particular dogs; but this has more to do with chance than any other condition. It's therefore unrealistic to expect anyone with canine allergies to live comfortably with a dog.

If someone who doesn't live with you suffers from allergies, potential discomfort may be minimized by a thorough vacuuming and airing of the home, and sequestering your dog for the duration of the luncheon or dinner party. Bear in mind as well that certain individuals may simply be frightened of dogs, either on principle or as a result of past experience. In such cases, it may be wise to keep your pet outside or in another room while you are entertaining; if your guest feels comfortable, you may attempt a gentle, gradual introduction. Many times, a formal introduction may be just as necessary for your dog, since he may feel nervous or threatened by someone who instinctively recoils from him.

Single people, meanwhile, face the possibility of commencing relations with a partner who is allergic to dogs, or who perhaps does not share an enthusiasm for things canine. Delicate situations of this nature are not typically resolved by clinging to the motto

"Love me, love my dog." Before you adopt a dog, consider your honest response to the prospect of choosing between human and canine love. You'll spare yourself, your partner, and your pet a great deal of agony.

IS IT REALLY A DOG WE WANT?

Even the most reliable individual may not be willing or able to offer the kind of care and attention a dog truly needs. This should not be considered a condemnation of any sort. Dogs depend on their owners to fulfill the most basic needs; and despite their sympathy toward human affairs, they remain, at heart, wild creatures. It may not be possible to articulate the fundamental difference between dogs and people, but it cannot be ignored.

Some household pets, such as mice, turtles, and fish, thrive only in specifically confined environments. Even a cat can happily spend its days in a studio apartment. Dogs, however, need to move about—even if their exploration only takes them around the block. To deny a dog this freedom is to deny an essential part of its nature. Don't even contemplate getting a dog if taking a stroll around the block three times a day doesn't appeal to you.

Moreover, as pack animals, dogs will instinctively assume a dominant position unless deliberately conditioned to submit to a higher authority. The effort required to instill discipline is usually far greater than imagined. Consistency is essential, and a fine line between severity and compassion must be observed at all times. Though dogs possess a high degree of intelligence and sensitivity, maintaining good, orderly conduct will be a lifelong occupation for you. In certain cases, it may never be completely effective: Either through temperament or ineffective early training, some dogs cannot wholeheartedly submit.

A QUESTIONNAIRE

If you're still wondering whether having a dog is right for you, you might find it helpful to examine the following questionnaire. It is not intended to test your competence, but merely to shed light on your attitudes and expectations so that you can answer the essential question: Should we have a dog?

1. If the eager, cuddly puppy who broke your heart in the store window turns into a stubborn little demon at home,

will you throw in the towel? What if your dog turns out to be aggressive?

2. Can you devise a rational plan of action when he swallows a golf ball or a bar of decorative soap?

3. Can you deal with the occasional broken vase or dog hair on your suits and sweaters? What is your attitude toward owning a collection of left shoes?

4. Can you put someone else's needs before your own? At the end of a long day, will you go back to the car and drive to the nearest grocery store if there's no puppy chow in the house?

5. How do you really feel about picking up two or three times your own weight in canine droppings every year?

6. Do you spend a lot of time away on business or vacation? Could you be transferred to a foreign country that might refuse to admit dogs or require a long quarantine?

7. If you don't own your current residence, does the owner or landlord allow dogs?

8. Does someone you live with suffer from allergies or other ailments? What about close friends or relatives?

9. Can you afford food, regular immunizations, and veterinarian visits? Is your budget flexible enough to allow for medical treatments in case of an accident or serious illness?

10. Finally, can you sustain a relationship for the next ten or twenty years? Do you think you might get bored when your dog is no longer peppy? When she's old and wobbly and her joints are sore and her eyesight fails, will you enjoy her company as much as when she was a puppy?

While the issues raised here are not conclusive, a majority of doubtful responses suggests that a dog is not an appropriate companion. Temperament or personal circumstances may incline you toward another kind of pet; perhaps it's only a matter of timing, and at some future point you'll find yourself better suited to accept the responsibilities of life with a dog. If, on the other hand, you feel reasonably secure about entering into a canine relationship, by all means proceed to Chapter Two.

Chapter 2

Yes, We Should Have a Dog!

If you hear a faint barking sound in the background right now, don't be alarmed: It's a canine chorus commending your generosity, perspicacity, and courage. For all three to reside in a single heart is a comparatively rare phenomenon, and you certainly deserve praise. After realistically contemplating the responsibilities involved in owning a dog, you have decided to go ahead with the adoption process. This is by no means an easy decision, and reflects a certain sobriety on your part.

If there were only one type of dog on earth, the next step would be relatively simple. Once you'd prepared your home for the new arrival, you'd merely have to locate an available dog. Unfortunately, few of life's operations arrange themselves so conveniently. With more than three hundred distinct breeds on record—and a host of animals whose genealogies may be described as more or less indeterminate—selecting the one that best suits your own temperament and expectations usually requires a bit of reflection. Among the items you may wish to consider are:

- Your own personality
- The canine qualities you especially esteem
- Breed-specific qualities
- The dog's individual history

WHAT KIND OF OWNER ARE YOU?

Most people imagine themselves as the Perfect Owner: kind, patient, generous, and magically resilient to accumulations of dog hair. Their daydreams of walking Jasper or Sadie are miraculously free of rain or snow, and never seem to take place before six in the morning. They are perfectly in synch with their pet, enjoying the same moods, the same energy level, and the same requirements of space, comfort, and society. More than one owner has adopted a dog on the strength of such wishful thinking alone.

Like all fantasies, however, the fantasy of the Perfect Owner leaves little room for surprise—and life with a real four-footed furry creature is nothing if not full of surprises. Most of them are quite pleasant, of course. Silly tricks and impromptu dog behavior can form the basis of memories treasured for years; when you're at a loss, your dog can offer you a look of such profound confidence and understanding, you'd swear he was more evolved than most humans ever pretend to be. Then again, he may eat something that doesn't agree with him, and the surprise will appear somewhat less charming, if no less memorable. Ultimately, no matter what type of owner you would like to be, you need to allow room for spontaneity in your relationship with your pet. If you can do so, chances are you'll find in him or her a wonderful guide to living fully in the present moment.

Of course, the level of spontaneity you can reasonably handle largely depends on your situation and personal habits. You may, for instance, thrive only in a tightly organized living environment, or you may take a more casual approach to housekeeping. Perhaps you prefer outdoor activities to indoor pastimes, or enjoy a quiet afternoon in front of the fireplace to an hour or so of chasing crows. Your home may consist of one room or twenty. Your age, strength, and stamina are equally important. Since walking, grooming, and playing require physical interaction with your pet, you will ultimately feel more secure handling a dog whose size is appropriate to your physical abilities. If every walk escalates into a tug of war, and bath time leaves you soggier than Rover, you may become disenchanted rather quickly.

As mentioned in Chapter One, your daily schedule needs to be considered. No matter what their size and temperament, all dogs require at least some degree of personal attention, so you need to determine the amount of time you can realistically devote to your pet's needs. At the end of the day, you may want nothing better than to fall into a hot bath or a cold martini, but try explaining that to someone who has been waiting all day just to play with you. If your schedule is full or erratic, you may want to choose a dog that does not require a high degree of maintenance, such as a Welsh corgi or a Boston terrier.

WHAT ARE YOU LOOKING FOR IN A DOG?

The incredible diversity of dog breeds stems from a certain degree of specialization within each bloodline. Some dogs excel at hunting, for example, while others prefer to retrieve. Some enjoy nothing more than bullying a herd of sheep or cattle; others rule the household while safely enthroned on their owner's lap. The beagle's friendliness suits him for busy households, but he is unlikely to present much of a deterrent to intruders. Dalmatians, meanwhile, thrive in the company of outdoor enthusiasts, but tend to become spiteful if kept indoors too long.

Before deciding on the type of animal you want, it's wise to make a list of qualities important to you. Although temperament may vary somewhat with each individual dog, purebreds can be reasonably expected to conform to the standards to which they have been bred. Even in the case of a mixed heritage, one or two specific characteristics usually dominate. Chapter Three will examine canine characteristics by breed, and you may wish to supplement this information by consulting veterinarians, other owners, and breeders. Even so, a few general distinctions may prove useful at this point.

Frisky Puppies or Responsible Adults?

Puppies are among the most adorable creatures on earth—eager, cuddly, loving, and absolutely devoted to their new owners. Most of them enjoy handling, too, which makes them eminently suitable for children; and pets adopted at a very young age usually develop a close, affectionate bond with their human families. However, puppies need an enormous amount of love and attention, since the sudden departure from the warmth and familiarity of parents and litter mates can often provoke anxiety and confusion. Moreover, housebreaking and training must begin from the ground up, demanding an unimaginable amount of time and patient effort. Finally, puppyhood represents a mere fraction of a dog's life. By the age of twenty weeks, he's a gangly adolescent—still lovable, of course, but rather more cumbersome.

Older dogs, though perhaps less immediately endearing than puppies, are often housebroken and are able to understand basic commands. Unfortunately, the effects of bad or inconsistent early training may be difficult to reverse, and attempts to do so may cause a good deal of frustration for both you and an adult pet.

Still, a dog's character is fully realized by the time he's a year old, and after interacting with an adult for a little while, you should be able to determine whether or not you get along.

Familiarity with the environment in which the dog was raised can help you to predict his behavior to some degree, and thereby provide a guide for correcting troublesome behavior. You're less likely to know much about an animal adopted from a pound or shelter; yet dogs rescued from certain death often return the gift of freedom with love, loyalty, and devotion. In a sense, while a dog you raise from puppyhood will probably always seem like a child in your eyes, an older dog may feel more like a faithful companion or confidant.

Athlete or Aesthete?

In your heart of hearts, do you see yourself reading the paper in front of a fireplace while your dog sleeps peacefully on the hearth? If so, then perhaps you'll be happier with a dog who has a placid disposition, doesn't require too much exercise or attention, and is content to simply rest wherever you are. You might consider adopting a bulldog, a French mastiff, a Saint Bernard, or a pinscher. These breeds require less exercise than many others, and their temperament is usually relaxed and comforting.

More active persons, or those who enjoy spending time outdoors, may prefer a dog who likes a good deal of exercise in the open air. Whippets, for example, are insatiable runners, while greyhounds love to accompany their owners on hikes, bicycle rides, or morning jogs. Few golden retrievers, meanwhile, will ever pass up the chance to chase a stick or a ball and bring it back so it can be thrown again. And again. And again.

Colossal or Compact?

Most big dogs have a lot in common with big people. They are generally unhappy in cramped quarters, and prefer wide-open areas in which to stretch, exercise, or simply ramble about showing off their muscles. If you wouldn't mind sharing your home with a handsome, strapping creature, you might want to consider an Akita, Irish wolfhound, or Newfoundland—providing, of course, your home is large enough to accommodate both of you comfortably. Bear in mind, too, that large dogs are quite strong and require a firm hand in training; even if Kobo has mild manners, you'll still need to prove you're strong enough to handle him.

On the other hand, you may prefer a somewhat less obtrusive presence in your abode. Perhaps your physical condition is such that you would need a dog that is small and light enough for you to carry. In this case, you might want to look at a toy spaniel. Small dogs adapt more easily to confined spaces than their larger brothers and sisters, and they never seem to lose that puppyish quality. There is something inherently adorable about even the most ancient Chihuahua.

Prince or Peasant?

Since pedigreed animals are carefully bred to produce distinct physical and emotional characteristics, their habits can be predicted with greater certainty than those of dogs whose heritage is more ambiguous. Moreover, breeders typically allow prospective buyers to visit their kennels. Whether you are adopting a purebred or not, an opportunity of this kind should be grasped without hesitation, since a dog's permanent attitude toward people is often determined by the manner in which he is handled as a puppy. Meanwhile, because character traits are often passed down from dog to puppy, the chance to observe one or both canine parents may also indicate something of your prospective puppy's character.

Naturally, pure stock does not guarantee sound mind and body. Many regal lines suffer from a streak of madness or congenital defect. Pedigreed dogs also tend to be more expensive than humbler varieties, especially if the dog you've chosen comes from a long line of prize winners. If you decide to show your dog, you can expect costs to rise even more dramatically, since additional grooming and training, not to mention entering and traveling to shows, constitutes an investment that may range from the merely astonishing to the truly staggering.

The obvious advantage in adopting a mixed-breed dog has to do with a lower initial investment. In general, a mixed-breed dog can be acquired for no more than the cost of her initial vaccinations and worming. Many animal shelters even arrange with local veterinarians for a free initial visit or free neutering. Moreover, mixed-breed animals tend to be healthier and more emotionally stable than pedigrees. A casual glance through any supermarket tabloid should offer proof enough of the sad state of modern nobility.

Of course, just because your puppy can't say for sure who his parents are doesn't mean he won't manifest his share of peculiarities. Should you decide to adopt a mixed-breed dog, make every attempt to visit his home environment and observe his interactions with the other members of the household. If you're adopting a dog from a shelter or pet store, find out as much as you can about his parents and previous owners. Since dogs rarely seek psychiatric counseling, they are usually unequipped to articulate their own natures. It's up to you to gather as much information as you can about your dog.

Male or Female?

A mythology of gender difference pervades human culture, giving rise to some peculiarly disturbing notions. It is rumored, for example, that female dogs bond more closely to male owners, and vice versa. Male dogs are thought to exhibit greater emotional stability than females, while the latter are assumed to be capable of deeper devotion. Twaddle of this sort colors even the terms used to distinguish male and female dogs: The former are simply called males—or, less commonly, "studs"—while females are referred to even in polite conversation as "bitches."

Certain biological differences cannot be denied, of course, and you may wish to take these into account. Instinct compels male dogs to mark their territory by squirting a small amount of urine at regular intervals, and to investigate all traces left by other dogs and animals. Walking a male thus requires more patience on your part than walking a female.

Females, meanwhile, typically enter a period of heightened sexual tension twice a year, which may last several days. During this period, temptation may inspire any number of imprudent behaviors, such as leaping fences and roaming back alleys in search of pleasure. Females in this state (commonly referred to as "heat") emit a particular scent, which, though undetectable to the human nose, exerts a powerful influence over male dogs. Once this scent is recognized, males tend to lose all sense of dignity, and will need to be restrained just as vigorously as females. Problems of this sort can only be resolved by neutering or spaying. These operations are highly recommended, and will be discussed in more detail in Chapter Six.

Choosing a Healthy Dog

Though it is not impossible to see a friend or neighbor walking a three-legged dog, caring for a pet whose life has been compromised by illness or injury often requires greater commitment than normally observed. It may also require a substantial investment of time, money, and personal strength. The affection these dogs can show in return often exceeds the effort that goes into caring for them. And while every dog must succumb to some form of biological misfortune, persons who willingly adopt a sick or injured animal should be counted among the true heroes of our age.

Understandably, most people seek a companion with whom they can share several years of mutual affection. Accordingly, whether your ideal dog is large or small, active or placid, male or female, keep an eye out for the following signs of physical well-being when making your selection:

- Alert, responsive behavior
- A shiny coat
- Clear, bright eyes
- A clean, cool nose
- Clean ears
- Pale pink gums and tongue
- White teeth
- A clean bottom
- A firm belly

Likewise, the following symptoms may indicate illness, abuse, or neglect:

- Nervousness or shyness
- Snarling, growling, hackles, or hard biting
- Sneezing or coughing
- Discharge from the eyes, nose, or ears
- Potbelly
- Bald patches or dull fur
- Lumps or skin rashes
- Yellow or missing teeth
- Twitching, constant tilting, or shaking of the head

An individual dog who exhibits any of these symptoms should probably be avoided, unless you're willing to spend the time and money restoring him to health. If you're selecting from a litter or group, be sure to examine each animal closely. Should one appear unhealthy, you're probably better off choosing your companion elsewhere. Several infectious diseases, as well as a number of common parasites, can be easily transmitted between dogs; so even if the animal you're considering shows every sign of radiant health, potential diseases may not have progressed beyond the incubation stage. Discovering that you have adopted a sick dog can be heartbreaking, particularly for children.

In addition, certain breeds are genetically prone to specific health problems, such as hip dysplasia, heart defects, and retinal degeneration. These and other breed-related maladies will be treated in Chapter Three. Most responsible breeders make every effort to insure that unfavorable genetic tendencies are not passed down. It is virtually impossible, however, to suppress a wayward chromosome permanently, and animals purchased in pet stores are rarely screened as thoroughly as those acquired directly from a responsible breeder. Before adopting any purebred, therefore, you are advised to discover as much as you can about potential hereditary defects associated with the breed. You should also discuss the possibility of returning or replacing the animal, should any serious problems come to light within a few weeks of adoption.

WHERE DO DOGS COME FROM?

Sources of adoption vary according to region and availability. In general, they may be classified under the following headings:

- Homes
- Breeders
- Shelters
- Pet stores
- Veterinarians

Strays, of course, tend to enter one's life quite by chance, and thus can't be said to derive from any particular source. Since strays are often unfortunate victims of human cruelty, they require special consideration and will be discussed separately, at the end of this section.

Homes

Responsible dog owners neuter or spay sexually mature pets (as mentioned earlier, this will be discussed in Chapter Six). Regrettably, some either delay the operation, or forgo it entirely in the belief that allowing their pets to suffer periodic states of extreme agitation is somehow kinder or more natural. Both attitudes contribute to a lamentable increase in the number of unwanted dogs. Unless you've set your heart on a particular breed, you might ask your friends, neighbors, or colleagues if they know of anyone seeking a good home for a puppy or adult dog. In addition, many pet stores, shelters, and veterinarian's offices often post adoption notices, as may libraries, community centers, or other public areas. Local newspapers frequently advertise pet sales or adoptions.

Direct-from-home adoptions offer a number of advantages to the prospective buyer. Simply observing a dog in her familiar surroundings can provide insight into her overall health and personality, while the chance to play with her at some length can help determine your compatibility. There is, after all, a great deal to be said for chemistry. Home visits also afford you the opportunity to study the way your prospective friend interacts with other members of the household, as well as with furniture, plants, and other domestic ornaments. If you're choosing a puppy from a litter, it's a good idea to spend some time with each one. Though the sturdy little chap who marches straight up to you and smilingly nips your ankle may be the first to catch your eye, the shy girl in the corner may be the one who ultimately melts your heart. As a rule, though, overtly aggressive or timid animals make difficult pets.

Mixed-breed dogs and puppies can usually be acquired free of charge, or for the cost of any prior immunization, worming, or other treatments. Not all owners go to the trouble of immunizing their little ones, so you'll need to ask directly. If little Lulu has been vaccinated, ask for a receipt or statement from the veterinarian. In fact, you should request all paperwork relating to the dog's medical history. If it's not available, request the name and number of her veterinarian, from whom you can usually obtain copies of important records. If the owner has never taken her to a vet, you may want to consider looking elsewhere. Undetected medical problems may cause you grief in the near future.

Breeders

As mentioned earlier, purebred dogs tend to cost more than mixed breeds. Price varies according to the rarity or popularity of the breed, the glamour of the lineage, and the margin of profit an individual breeder has determined. Untrustworthy breeders, meanwhile, undermine the fine work done by more responsible individuals and organizations, who go to great lengths to ensure the health and genetic purity of each new litter. It pays, therefore, to investigate. You may wish to consult veterinarians or your local ASPCA, or attend a dog show and talk with owners of the type of dog you have in mind.

For information regarding responsible breeders in your area, you may also contact the American Kennel Club (AKC) or the United Kennel Club (UKC). While both organizations recognize many of the same breeds, certain breeds are recognized only by one or the other club. The addresses of both organizations are listed in Appendix A. In addition, a number of breeders and kennel clubs maintain sites on the World Wide Web. Acme Pet offers a list of sites at http://www.acmepet.com/canine/market/k9__bre.html. Or you can simply use a search engine or directory.

Should you contemplate showing your dog, you must ascertain beforehand whether it meets the requirements established by either the AKC or UKC. In general, for a dog to be registered with either organization, both its parents must also be registered. For more specific guidelines, contact the American Kennel Club at:

The American Kennel Club
51 Madison Avenue
New York, NY 10010
http://www.akc.org

Or contact the United Kennel Club at:

The United Kennel Club
100 East Kilgore Road
Kalamazoo, MI 49001

As of early 1997, the UKC did not have its own Web site. However, information could be obtained at the following Internet address: http://www.ptialaska.net/~pkalbaug/ukcindex.html.

Every month, the AKC publishes the *AKC Gazette: The Official Journal for the Sport of Purebred Dogs*; the UKC, meanwhile, publishes several magazines, including *Bloodlines*, which covers information on most breeds recognized by the organization. Upcoming shows are announced in these and other magazines dedicated to fans of purebred dogs. If your local library or bookstore doesn't carry these publications, contact information is listed in Appendix A.

Even if you don't intend to show your dog, you should definitely ask for her registration certificate (also referred to as a pedigree or papers). This certificate will verify her lineage, and is absolutely essential should you someday decide to breed her.

Shelters

Adopting a dog from a shelter or pound is the mark of a truly humane individual. Abandoned animals desperately need homes, and unless they've suffered systematic abuse, will usually reward adoptive owners with untold amounts of gratitude and devotion. Nor are all shelter dogs mature animals; whole litters of puppies are regularly dropped off by owners who are either frustrated by their own attempts to find a home for the darlings, or just can't be bothered. More often than not, they're the same individuals who don't trouble to neuter their pets (and they will pay dearly for their neglect on the other side). Conversely, those who adopt one or more pets from a shelter will almost certainly introduce a substantial quantity of merit into their stream of being.

Dogs of all sorts can end up in a shelter. Some are saved from a squalid life in back alleys and on street corners, while others may have formerly belonged to loving owners who have either died or become unable to care for them. Though a large percentage come from mixed stock, it is not uncommon to find purebreds rescued from disreputable or neglectful breeders. While the details of a dog's history will probably not fill an entire page, shelter workers routinely examine, immunize, and worm all animals admitted to their facilities; so you can reasonably expect to adopt a healthy pet. Only very young puppies are not routinely immunized, since vaccinations typically can't be given before the age of eight weeks.

The cost of adoption is often minimal, usually covering vaccinations and paperwork, which may be offset in part by special arrangements for an introductory veterinary exam or free neutering. While most pounds and shelters are listed in the telephone book, you may wish to contact the Humane Society of the United States or the American Society for the Prevention of Cruelty to Animals (ASPCA), as listed below:

The Humane Society of the United States
2100 L Street NW
Washington, DC 20037
(202) 452-1100

·ASPCA
424 East 92nd Street
New York, NY 10128
(212) 876-7700·

Pet Stores

Pet store owners frequently fill their front windows with adorable
puppies, all wriggling enthusiastically or staring winsomely at
passersby. While many shop managers do so out of the purest
intentions, the ingenuity of such a marketing ploy cannot be denied. The type of people inclined to stand raptly by the window
making eccentric noises and unseemly faces are almost always
the same ones who will buy a dog on impulse.

Should you find yourself drawn toward spontaneous adoption,
you must take steps to protect yourself. At all costs, refrain from
instantly demanding to hold one of the animals, and instead spend
a few minutes wandering up and down the aisles. Inspect the store
for cleanliness and organization. Noxious odors, open bags of
food and other items, and parasitic animals sidling about the floor
should alert you to the possibility of an indifferent or neglectful
manager, who would not flinch at the thought of selling a diseased
or otherwise distressed animal.

Only after you've examined the store should you take a closer
look at the animals in the window. Spend a while watching them
interact with one another, and scrutinize them for signs of health
or illness. Observe, too, the condition of the cage or pen in which
they're kept. A dirty or foul-smelling cage often indicates neglect.

If the store looks tidy and well organized, and the dogs on
display seem healthy and enthusiastic, talk to the salespeople. The
presence of surly or uninformed help does not usually promise
an auspicious transaction. If the people you speak with appear
knowledgeable, ask about the diet and medical history of the dog
who interests you particularly, and gather as much information as
possible about its origins. If you are contemplating a purebred,
make sure it comes with papers. If papers aren't available, it's
probably not a purebred. This is not a tragedy in itself, but it
would seem to call the integrity of the management into question.

Finally, find out if the store offers any sort of guarantee. If so,
read it over carefully; it may be worth somewhat less than the
paper it's printed on. Many so-called guarantees offer only limited

veterinary care if the animal becomes ill within a specified period. In addition, you may not be entitled to a full refund should you decide to return a sick or behaviorally disturbed dog. At best, you may be able to exchange him for another dog of the same breed.

Veterinarians

While veterinarians frequently allow dog owners to post adoption notices in their offices, this should not be considered an endorsement of either the dog's health or the owner's trustworthiness. If the office receptionist is not preoccupied, you might inquire politely if the advertised dog is a patient. A positive answer would no doubt be encouraging, and may be followed by a polite request to arrange an appointment with the doctor to discuss the animal. In addition, some veterinarians occasionally shelter stray or abandoned animals; in which case, you may reasonably expect the dog or puppy to enjoy sound health. Since he will likely have developed a cordial relationship with the vet, you won't have to worry overmuch about resistance to yearly physicals and other medical visits.

A Few Words About Strays

Always approach a stray dog with caution. The early stages of rabies are not always apparent, and if you're bitten—even scratched or licked—by a rabid animal who exhibits no obvious symptoms, you will almost certainly die. Rabid dogs tend to act a little peculiar, though. They may seem overly affectionate when fear or caginess would be the proper response, or they may appear dazed or clumsy. Probably the most common signs of advanced rabies are twitching, persistent snapping, and foaming at the mouth. Dogs exhibiting such behavior should be avoided at all costs and reported immediately to the local ASPCA, police station, or sheriff's office.

Dogs born in the wild, meanwhile, tend to possess a savage streak, and may very well attack when approached. Though any dog will likely display some initial wariness, if a stray growls, snarls, barks excessively, or raises his hackles, you'd best give up any thought of contact. Back away slowly until you're at a safe distance, and contact the ASPCA or a local rescue organization as soon as you can.

If, however, a stray responds favorably to your approach, and after a few minutes of sniffing and tail wagging decides to let you touch him, your first duty is to ascertain whether or not he is wearing a tag. If so, contact his rightful owners immediately. If not, you should bring him to a pound or shelter right away; if he's merely slipped out of his collar, his owners will likely contact every institution in the area.

If you're bent on adopting him, you can make arrangements with the pound or shelter to retrieve him after a certain period has elapsed. This will not only give his real family time to locate him, but also allow you an opportunity to consider your impulse a bit more rationally. After all, you know nothing about him, and he may not be the appropriate companion for you. Should you ultimately decide to adopt him, you will need to make vaccination and license arrangements with the facility to which you've brought him, and afterwards bring him around to the vet for a complete physical examination. It may seem like an awful lot of trouble to go through for a complete stranger, but you'll rest more comfortably at night knowing you've done everything you can to ensure his safety and your own.

WHERE CAN WE FIND OUT MORE?

The true mystery of the canine can never be entirely fathomed. He is both fierce and tender, devoted and proud; though content to dwell in human settlements, his wild heart will not yield completely. Little wonder he has been an object of fascination and veneration for more than ten thousand years. Though the bond between dog and master is primarily one of passion, it is only reasonable to want to know as much as possible about your prospective dog. Especially if you're considering a purebred, you may wish to address specific concerns about temperament or illness; or you may need help choosing between one or another particular breed. Fortunately, detailed information may be obtained from a variety of reliable sources.

Other Owners probably represent the most reliable resource for questions concerning daily life with a canine companion. Since experience varies from individual to individual, you will undoubtedly hear more than a few contradictory stories. Still, the chance to discuss both mundane and extraordinary issues with several different people should present you with a fairly balanced idea of the vicissitudes of dog-rearing.

Books and Magazines offer meticulous advice on nearly every facet of canine care—from electric fences to natural diets. Depending on the size of your local library or bookshop, the selection of dog-related books may occupy an entire wall or merely part of a shelf. In general, books cover major subjects like training or showing in explicit detail. Magazines, on the other hand, typically supply up-to-the-minute information on topics ranging from canine dentistry to travel tips.

CD-ROMs and Videotapes achieve the stupendous feat of presenting important information in an entertaining fashion. Though sometimes sketchy in detail, multimedia offerings more than compensate with lively footage of the proper approach to canine bathing or the most effective means of convincing a Chihuahua to leap through Mother's embroidery hoop.

The Internet has evolved into a prodigious source of information on almost any subject imaginable. Armed with a computer, a modem, and an Internet Service Provider, you can browse the World Wide Web for answers and advice on a huge variety of canine-related matters. Although Internet sites appear and vanish with maddening frequency, you might try your luck with The American Kennel Club, located at www.akc.org/; Dog-e-zine, at www.dog-e-zine.com/; or Acme Pet at www.acmepet.com/canine/. Online services such as CompuServe and America Online also sponsor forums for pet owners. Posting questions and reading messages in Usenet newsgroups, meanwhile, offers another means of learning more about dogs. Like Web pages, newsgroups come and go, but rec.pets.dogs seems to have enjoyed a certain longevity.

Dog Shows are vastly entertaining, even to those who don't profess a genuine interest in dogs. Any opportunity to observe dogs leap, dance, and display various attitudes of obedience will serve not only to highlight the truly remarkable canine capacity to listen to and understand their owners, but also to point out the enormous variety among dogs of a particular breed. In addition, proud owners tend to be preternaturally forthcoming about the responsibilities and advantages of raising a particular kind of dog.

Kennel Clubs are responsible for organizing shows and for disseminating information on a particular breed or breeds. Most clubs are overseen by a dog registry, of which the two most prominent are the American Kennel Club and the United Kennel Club. Most local clubs are categorized according to breed. If you can't find a listing for a club in your area, ask your veterinarian or local animal shelter for suggestions. Otherwise, you can contact one of the registries listed in Appendix A.

THE ROLE OF INSTINCT

Selecting the most appropriate dog for your household necessarily involves a good deal of deliberation. Strain should be avoided, however. In this world, perfection is a relative measure rather than an absolute one, and your darling Angus or Lucy is certain to engage in reprehensible behavior on occasion. A life shared with another creature is necessarily a balance between grace and disappointment, and to presume otherwise can only lead to unhealthy psychological states.

Likewise, no amount of study can make up for actual experience. All the books in the world and all the advice you glean from owners is still only commentary, and can't approach the real drama of a direct encounter with a living, breathing dog. As you're about to make a final choice from among a litter of rumbustious terriers, you may spy a rugged old warrior in the background. Wobbling closer on three legs, he cracks a crooked smile at you. His breath is ghastly, but the warmth of it on your cheek reminds you of things you haven't thought about since childhood. Suddenly, your patient research pales in significance.

Such is the strange magic a dog can work on the human heart. Its power is not to be denied, nor its glory diminished in any way by a humble appearance. If you truly want to know why dog owners go to such great lengths for their pets, and why they seem to rattle on so passionately about their virtues, then sink your hands in a bundle of living fur and gaze into a pair of eyes that gives clarity new meaning. The experience, most likely, will transcend all commentary.

Chapter 3

The Possible Puppy

After some consideration, you've probably made some decisions about the type of dog you'd like. Perhaps a fine large fellow with a mellow disposition strikes your fancy. Or maybe you've settled on a small sort who enjoys more attention without taxing your strength. Possibly you're pulled toward the middle way: a companion who is neither too large, nor too small; neither highly active, nor decidedly lethargic. Or you may yearn for an exotic creature who will turn heads as you walk down the street together.

The good news is, with well over one hundred purebred animals to choose from, and countless mixed varieties, you're likely to find a pet who matches your ideal fairly precisely. The bad news is, with well over one hundred purebred animals to choose from, and countless mixed varieties, your search could take a very long time.

BREED CATEGORIES

Canine registries such as the AKC and the UKC have striven to bring a sense of order to this somewhat perplexing diversity by categorizing breeds according to function. Most of the breeds in evidence today were originally bred to fit certain tasks. These included flushing game from their nests, tracking criminals, and perching attractively on milady's lap while milord was otherwise engaged.

Today, most registries recognize seven different categories of dog breeds. Some registries may combine two categories, or may refuse to recognize particular breeds within a specific group. This failure to adopt absolute standards, though at times confusing, at least avoids the worst excesses of social tyranny. Should a breed be ostracized by one registry, another may graciously decide to offer membership. The basic categories are described below.

Sporting Dogs

Often referred to as bird dogs, gun dogs, or hunting dogs, the breeds included in this group are characterized by a high degree of energy, a passion for exercise, and a capacity to withstand weather conditions that keep most sensible people indoors. As a general rule, they are muscular enough to endure long hours of tramping through woods and fields with their masters, while their tough coats protect them from cold, damp, brambles, thorns, and other unpleasant natural phenomena. Sporting dogs include the following breeds:

- Pointers
- Setters
- Retrievers
- Spaniels

as well as

- Vizslas
- Weimaraners
- Wirehaired pointing griffons

Each breed tends to excel at certain tasks. Pointers, for example, run ahead of the hunter to locate quarry; when they find it, they pose rigidly with one foot raised and tail standing out in a straight line. Not unreasonably, such behavior is called "pointing." While setters also specialize in locating game, their preferred method of signaling the location of a plump partridge or handsome quail is to sink silently to the ground, or "set."

Spaniels, meanwhile, were developed to flush game from their dens or hiding places, and drive them toward waiting hunters—which does not seem especially sporting. Retrievers, on the other hand, stay close by their masters, take note of where the prey falls after being shot, and fetch it on command. In addition, certain breeds may combine specialities, such as flushing and pointing, while others exhibit particular strengths. The size of the weimaraner, for instance, suits him for hunting large game, while the lean, speedy vizsla is equally happy tracking waterfowl or terrorizing rabbits.

As might be expected, sporting dogs require a great deal of exercise, and will become restlessly destructive if confined inside a small apartment for too long. They have hearty appetites, and incline toward obesity if not allowed to run. A number of them make excellent watchdogs. However, because sporting dogs are by nature strong-willed, training must be undertaken early and with a very firm hand. Halfhearted attempts will produce an aggressive, potentially fierce animal.

Hounds

While sporting dogs merely assist hunters, hounds prefer to take charge themselves. They go after quarry with a relentlessness matched only by deficit hawks and telemarketers. It's not advisable, therefore, to adopt a hound if you own other types of small pets, such as cats, rabbits, chinchillas, or guinea pigs. Hounds have been bred to hunt down and kill small, foreign creatures. While exceptions no doubt exist, no amount of training can adequately convince a hound to accept Mr. Fuzzy as his stepbrother.

Many breeds in the hound category may be recognized simply by the word ''hound'' attached to their names. These include:

* Basset hounds
* Bloodhounds
* Coonhounds
* Foxhounds
* Greyhounds
* Irish wolfhounds

The dachshund may be a bit harder to recognize in this way, because the name has retained its German flavor. *Hund* is the German word for hound or dog, while *dachs* refers to the prey this stouthearted fellow was bred to hunt—the crafty badger. While Afghan hounds are often simply called Afghans, other breeds prefer even more anonymity. These include:

* Basenjis
* Beagles
* Borzois
* Harriers

- Salukis
- Whippets

Certain breeds, such as Afghans, display a tendency toward aloofness, shying both from strangers and other dogs. Others, such as basset hounds, actively enjoy both canine and human companionship, and can usually withstand the sort of roughhousing typical of children. These distinctions in temperament are mirrored by differences in hunting technique. Sight hounds—the group to which Afghans belong—rely on visual cues to run down their prey; they are typically fast, long-legged animals. Scent hounds—a group that includes basset hounds, beagles, and foxhounds—are blessed with superior olfactory capabilities. They tend to see rather poorly, however, and must hunt in packs if they're to bring down their quarry with any degree of reliable success.

Like their sporting cousins, hounds tend to become restless if confined too long in cramped quarters. They're apt to exercise their prowess on household items that don't stand a chance of escape, such as sofas, slippers, and moderately expensive luggage. They may also bark a great deal for no apparent reason, and, if sufficiently bored by inactivity, may snap at visitors, passersby, and other dogs. Properly trained, however, they make obedient, affectionate house pets. Since breeds range in size from the giant Irish wolfhound to the diminutive dachshund, it should be fairly easy to find a hound to suit just about any home.

Working Dogs

The breeds included in this group were reared to perform a variety of tasks for their human masters. Many were specifically bred as guard dogs, while others specialize in pulling sleds, rescuing alpine climbers and exhausted swimmers, towing fishing nets, and carrying messages between boats. They are, of necessity, large animals, with splendid muscles and gargantuan appetites, and typically need ample living space. However, with the exception of sled dogs—which were bred for speed and endurance—most require only moderate exercise.

A working dog's need for space has less to do with a propensity to occupy the entire dining area or accidentally displace a bookcase than with a tendency to become irritable—and possibly aggressive—in claustrophobic conditions. Among the breeds least likely to enjoy living in a small apartment are:

- Akitas
- Alaskan malamutes
- Bernese mountain dogs
- Bullmastiffs
- Doberman pinschers
- Giant schnauzers
- Great Danes
- Newfoundlands
- Rottweilers
- Saint Bernards

If given an appropriate amount of exercise, the following breeds are somewhat more inclined to adapt to city life:

- American Eskimos
- Boxers
- Samoyeds

Due to their size and independent nature, working dogs must be rigorously trained, or they will dominate their owners. For this reason, they do not make ideal pets for first-time dog owners, or for those who lack the time, will, or patience for serious training. Harsh methods can't make up for backsliding on the owner's part, and will almost definitely provoke vicious retaliation. In general, the larger the dog, the more capable he is of causing grave damage to people, property, and other animals. This must be taken into account if you live in an area populated by large numbers of children. On no account should you allow a stranger, young or old, to approach a large dog, unless he encourages such behavior. Warning and welcoming signs will be discussed in Chapter Five.

Working dogs have been bred to take the initiative in a variety of situations. While this no doubt contributes to their reluctance to accept authority, once trained, they are remarkably eager to please and exceptionally devoted to their human families. They make ideal guard dogs and watchdogs, and though some breeds may feel less comfortable about expressing affection, they feel compassion toward people of all ages, sizes, and genders. Many tales of canine rescue feature working dogs in the hero's role.

Terriers

Originally developed to hunt vermin, terriers are persistent, courageous animals, who enjoy nothing so much as the chance to dig up a burrow of nasty little creatures and fight them to the death. Their tenacity also proves useful in hunting particularly resistant game, such as foxes, otters, and weasels. Terriers are energetic dogs, and need a good deal of intellectual and physical stimulation when living in areas where vermin, otters, and the like have wisely made themselves scarce.

Like hounds and working dogs, terriers were bred as much for initiative as for stamina. Fearless in confrontation, they exhibit a pronounced tendency to challenge other dogs, even those larger than themselves. While early socialization can temper such aggressiveness, all encounters between terriers and other dogs should be closely supervised. The jaws of a terrier may be considered one of the seven wonders of evolution: Even a small dog can clamp an unsuspecting ankle or slender neck with deadly force. Terriers thus make excellent watchdogs, apt to bark furiously at the sight of a turning doorknob or the sound of footsteps on the front porch, and to offer intruders a grievously unpleasant welcome.

Because terriers tend to perceive any show of aggression as an invitation to duel, training can present a ticklish problem. Fortunately, breeds in this group are by nature highly intelligent and inquisitive, so training may be handled as a test of skill, in which success is rewarded with toothsome treats. Daily exercise, meanwhile, should include a vigorous game of fetch. Not only will Princess be sorely disappointed by a mere jog around the block, she will likely take matters into her own hands by challenging your collection of antique porcelain dolls to a death match, or shredding your Great-aunt Ethel's sealskin coat.

Nevertheless, their intelligence and high spirits make terriers excellent family pets. They are especially handy with children, strong enough to withstand rough play, while typically small enough to cuddle or curl up with at night. So affectionate are most terrier breeds, and so persistent in the face of indifference or rebuff, they can win the hearts of even the most inhibited individuals. For this reason, terriers are often used to help emotionally disturbed children gain a sense of confidence and social connectedness.

Large of heart, terriers are typically compact of body, and therefore adapt quite well to small quarters and urban environments. Roughly half the breeds in this group are small dogs, and can fit quite comfortably in a studio or one-bedroom apartment. These include:

- Australian terriers
- Border terriers
- Bull terriers
- Cairn terriers
- Dandie Dinmont terriers
- Fox terriers
- Miniature schnauzers
- Norfolk terriers
- Norwich terriers
- Scottish terriers
- Sealyham terriers
- Skye terriers

Larger breeds include:

- Airedale terriers
- American Staffordshire terriers
- Kerry blue terriers
- Wheaten terriers

Regardless of size, however, virtually all terriers thrive best on a steady diet of affection and companionship.

Toys

While other breeds were developed to assist their masters in a variety of strenuous tasks, toys were bred for a single, comparatively casual, purpose: companionship. This does not mean, however, that toys are merely a contemporary luxury, bred for a society that enjoys more leisure than the industrious caveman. As a matter of fact, several toy breeds can proudly boast an ancient heritage. The Italian greyhound, for example, can trace its origins back two thousand years, while the pug line extends back even further, to around 400 B.C. Other breeds in this group include:

- Affenpinschers
- Brussels griffons

- Chihuahuas
- English toy spaniels
- Japanese chins
- Maltese
- Papillons
- Pekingese
- Pomeranians
- Pugs
- Shih tzus

as well as compact varieties of other breeds, including:

- English toy spaniels
- Toy Manchester terriers
- Miniature dachshunds
- Miniature pinschers
- Toy poodles
- Silky terriers
- Yorkshire terriers

Despite their diminutive size and adorable moniker, toys should not be confused with actual playthings. They are, for the most part, brilliant, energetic creatures, fully capable of manipulating their owners into performing an array of humble services on their behalf. In addition, because their physical structure is rather delicate, they can't withstand the rough treatment customarily reserved for dolls and other inanimate objects of affection. They do not make ideal pets for small children, therefore. And although they may look particularly precious perched high on a bed or on the arm of a chair, a sudden fall from grace may cause lasting injuries.

Toys do not consider themselves small. Confident and inquisitive, they will boldly approach much larger dogs, who might easily make a meal of an assertive shih tzu or Pomeranian, if not amused by its effrontery. Since toys are apt to take a bid for dominance quite seriously, social encounters with other canines require careful monitoring. Strangers are likewise subject to surprisingly aggressive scrutiny, and the sound of a doorbell or the casual approach of a passerby will usually set off a lively round of high-pitched yapping. Yet, though they make superb alarm dogs, most toys are physically unequal to the task of discouraging persons intent on mischief.

Toys can live quite happily in a small apartment, and fulfill their need for exercise with a few high-speed turns around the bedroom. However, they don't appreciate being left in a tiny room for long periods while their owners are at work or entertaining. They will not hesitate to vocalize their annoyance, raising the intensity and volume of their complaint until satisfaction is achieved. Such behavior is usually disagreeable to one's neighbors.

Owners must take steps to accustom their pets from an early age to periods of solitude. This may prove more difficult than imagined, since toys are unusually dependent on human companionship. While many breeds can be readily transported in a moderately sized handbag, and fit conveniently in the proper container under the seat of an airplane, owners should resist the temptation to bring their pets along on every outing. Otherwise, the first time little Rosalie is left on her own, you may come home to find a nasty petition from your neighbors pinned to your door.

Nonsporting Dogs

Despite the unfortunate title applied to this category, the breeds included here are not poor losers, and are no more likely to cheat at cards than the average dog. The name is meant to describe a number of breeds developed either solely for companionship, or for purposes they no longer serve. The category is necessarily diverse, and includes:

- Bichons frises
- Boston terriers
- Bulldogs
- Chow chows
- Dalmatians
- French bulldogs
- Keeshonden
- Lhasa apsos
- Poodles
- Shar-peis
- Schipperkes
- Tibetan terriers

Temperament, size, and appearance vary widely among members of this group. In general, however, they are alert, intelligent, and moderate in their dietary and exercise habits. Dalmatians tend to be more nervous than other nonsporting dogs, and require more vigorous exercise to burn off excess energy. Poodles, on the other hand, tend to be more even-tempered; though happiest in the company of humans, they won't suffer paroxysms of despair if left to their own devices while their owners are away from home eight or nine hours a day earning kibble money.

Many nonsporting breeds originally served in some capacity as watchdogs or guard dogs. On the whole, their modern descendants tend to regard strangers and other dogs with a moderate degree of suspicion. They may even display some reserve around their owners; yet this in no way reflects a lack of concern or loyalty. Nonsporting dogs are, as a rule, a fiercely devoted lot. With the possible exception of chow chows and shar-peis, whose stubborn streaks may require firmer handling, they all respond sensitively to training. While all members of this group make excellent family pets, chow chows may prove a bit too strong for persons with limited physical resources, and Dalmatians should be accustomed to children earlier on than most other dogs.

Herd Dogs

The forebears of the breeds in this category can be counted among the earliest domesticated dogs. Just as Stone Age hunters learned to appreciate canine assistance in bringing down prey, so the world's first farmers recognized a dog's value in controlling and protecting livestock. Long before enclosed meadows were feasible, herd dogs kept grazing yaks and goats from straying too far afield; at the end of the day, they leapt and barked around the ungrateful beasts, urging them home. Night and day, they kept watch against predators, often fighting powerful, ravenous animals to the death.

Good herd dogs needed vast reserves of stamina, and coats dense enough to protect them against cold, moisture, heat, burrs, and so forth. They were often obliged to act independently in the absence of their owners, and to respond immediately to the barest whiff of danger. Their modern descendants are therefore among the most sensitive and capable examples of the canine species, unswervingly devoted to their owners, and superbly responsive to training. However, puppies must be introduced to human society and their environments much earlier than those of other breed groups; otherwise aggressive and protective instincts may become unmanageable.

Herd dogs can be divided into two basic categories. The larger breeds typically performed their duties by circling their flocks, intimidating them by virtue of their size and by the alarming volume of their voices. Breeds in this category include:

- Belgian Malinois
- Belgian sheepdogs
- Belgian Tervuren
- Bouvier des Flandres
- Briards
- Collies
- German shepherds
- Old English sheepdogs

The second category of herd dogs include:

- Australian cattle dogs
- Bearded collies
- Pulis
- Shetland sheepdogs
- Welsh corgis

Smaller than their cousins, these breeds could not rely on size alone as a symbol of authority. In order to drive a reluctant herd out to pasture in the morning and back home at night, these dogs devised a method of jumping in and out among their charges, nipping at heels, barking, and creating a general impression of urgency. If only to avoid a swift kick in the teeth, dogs in this category tend to be quite nimble.

Although herd dogs continue to assist farmers and ranchers in many quarters of the world, modern technology has greatly reduced their utility. Understandably, several breeds in this category have chosen to seek employment elsewhere. Both the Bouvier des Flandres and the German shepherd have parlayed their skills into second careers as Seeing Eye dogs, and the latter have also enjoyed considerable success in the area of law enforcement. Many other breeds serve as watchdogs and guard dogs. Although urban life is acceptable if owners are willing to provide a thorough daily workout, herd dogs thrive in a suburban or rural environment, where they can run, bark, and pull rank on a variety of other creatures.

INDIVIDUAL CHARACTERISTICS

Selective breeding has never been an exact science. Character and ability vary widely among breeds within each of the categories outlined above. A bloodhound's nose, for example, is far superior to a greyhound's, but watching a pack of bloodhounds chase an electronic rabbit around a track would be rather a dull sport. Among working dogs, the giant schnauzer makes an excellent watchdog, but is typically friendly and affectionate toward people he knows. Dobermans, though superior guard dogs, may turn nasty if not trained by experienced handlers.

You're also apt to discover a variety of temperaments within every breed. Temperament stems, in part, from the efforts a breeder has made to discourage undesirable traits in the bloodline. No less important is early socialization, often referred to as imprinting. No matter how empathetic or human dogs may seem, they are bound by their animal nature; even the tiny Chihuahua can trace its roots to the primeval wolf. If dogs are to live comfortably in human society, a bond with people must be established very early on.

Even in spite of good breeding and early imprinting, though, individual dogs may depart wildly from the norms established for their breed. It is by no means impossible to come across a placid Rottweiler or a cranky otter hound. Depending on your own temperament, you may view such variation as a welcome opportunity to refine your search, or a stubborn refusal to conform.

Although selective breeding isn't foolproof, few would argue that some breeds are better at some things than others. Many people base their selection on one or more of these outstanding traits. Some of the most commonly considered abilities and characteristics will be discussed below, together with representative breeds. Even if you're considering a mixed breed, recognizing the qualities associated with her dominant bloodlines can help you understand her more deeply.

Watchdogs

It's a rare dog indeed who does not consider his home a kingdom. But unless his training has been carried out haphazardly, he won't usually cast himself in the role of king. Instead, he'll see himself as a kind of knight, upon whose prowess the safety of the kingdom and all who dwell within its borders depends. Like all good knights, he remains alert to the possibility of danger, and initially suspicious of even the most benevolent visitors.

A few breeds seem less inclined to assume an actively defensive role. Bloodhounds, for example, are more apt to console their quarry than to attack, and for this reason serve to track lost children and those who generally suffer from an impaired sense of direction. Irish wolfhounds trust strangers far too readily, although their gigantic stature may well dismay potential intruders. And though more fiercely protective than their adorable looks suggest, toys typically do not frighten persons intent on committing deeds that will earn them rebirth in the lower realms.

While almost all dogs take their territorial duties very seriously, several breeds outshine the rest. In general, these were bred specifically as watchdogs, serving to protect palaces, temples, and the influential persons who congregated there. Exceptionally vigilant, they tend to be a self-possessed lot, acutely aware of their strength and purpose. They must therefore be imprinted earlier than most, and trained with a firm hand. If you're looking for a watchdog, you may wish to consider one of the following breeds.

Akitas. These are large, muscular working dogs, with a very assertive temperament. Though perhaps too willful for most first-time dog owners, they make excellent companions if properly trained. Obedience school is recommended. Akitas need a great deal of exercise, are deeply attached to their owners, and interested in all aspects of home life. They won't stand for being ignored, and since adult dogs can weigh between seventy-five and one hundred pounds, owners must resign themselves to frequent and potentially embarrassing invasions of privacy. It may be useful to think of an Akita as a stereotypically overprotective mother, dressed in a thick fur coat with a large thick tail curled stylishly against the flank.

American Eskimos. This breed can trace its heritage back nearly six thousand years to the hunting dogs in the northern regions of present-day Europe. Over the centuries, its keen senses and powerful intelligence have been gradually turned away from the field and toward the home front. Though a bit too small to be a guard dog, the American Eskimo is a superb watchdog, staunchly committed to the protection of its family. Often mistaken for juvenile Samoyeds, Eskies have long, full coats, either pure white or cream-colored, and fluffy, curled tails. Only weekly brushing is required in cooler months; as the weather grows warmer, more frequent grooming is advised. Two types of Eskies are recognized. Miniatures stand ten to fifteen inches tall and weigh, on average, twelve to twenty pounds. Standards may grow between sixteen and twenty inches, and weigh between twenty and thirty-five pounds.

Irish Terriers. While all terriers make superb watchdogs, this particular breed tends to be more assertive than its cousins. Adults stand about eighteen inches tall and weigh between twenty-five and twenty-seven pounds, but their courage and fierce loyalty far exceed their size. These are alert, capable dogs, adaptable to any size environment, and usually quite benevolent toward children. Their dense, wiry coats range from bright red to pale beige, or wheaten. Like most terriers, they have long snouts, small dark eyes, and sensible beards; their ears flop delicately forward over the forehead.

Norwegian Elkhounds. Extremely protective, these animals seem to possess supernatural scent and hearing abilities. Their bark is shrill and piercing—a handy deterrent against intruders, though dogs of this breed should be trained to use their voices only when occasion warrants. Adults stand approximately twenty inches tall; they have compact, rectangular bodies, wedge-shaped heads, high-set ears, and thick, flat coats. Characteristically, their tails curl tightly against their backs.

Guard Dogs

People throughout the ages have used dogs for personal protection. Instinctively motivated to preserve the health and safety of their leaders, dogs make excellent bodyguards. Some guard dogs approach their duties more zealously than others, and should only be handled by experienced owners. Dobermans and pit bulls, for example, are among the most fiercely protective canines known. They should never be encouraged to attack, and the slightest impulse in that direction must be vigorously suppressed. Great personal authority and emotional stability are required to control these splendid animals. Perpetually tense and watchful, they are exceptionally unsuited to neighborhoods visited by children, cats, other dogs, postal workers, and anyone engaged in any sort of delivery service.

Most guard dogs are large, powerful creatures, and require

substantial amounts of exercise. They will not be satisfied by a daily jog around the corner, or the run of the backyard. Professional training is essential to keep these dogs in check. Their behavior toward strangers may range from simple aloofness to blatant hostility. Owners must take care to prevent casual acquaintances and well-meaning pedestrians from impulsively reaching out to pet a canine bodyguard. Around children, restraint is especially imperative; and though unsuspecting mothers may interpret a firm rebuff rather unkindly, most will prefer rejection to the horror of watching their child's hand swallowed whole.

Around their families, guard dogs tend to show less reserve. Many are demonstrably affectionate and gentle toward children they know. For this reason, most make excellent baby-sitters, and enjoy a reputation for rescuing children, the elderly, and the foolhardy from dangerous situations. Even so, do not even consider adopting a guard dog if you lack the means to send him to obedience school. With the possible exception of collies, most herd dogs make excellent bodyguards. Wary of strangers and frankly possessive, they are still capable of friendliness and sensibility. You may wish to look at one of the breeds below.

Australian Shepherds. These dogs enjoy being around their owners, while their herding instincts suit them to keep children from wandering too far or from coming into contact with suspicious creatures. They're built like collies, with round heads, tapering snouts, and medium-length coats that require brushing twice a week. Their muscular bodies are generally longer than they are tall. Energetic, nimble, and resourceful, they prefer working on a farm or ranch, but can easily adapt to suburban life if given sufficient stimulation.

Belgian Sheepdogs and Belgian Tervurens. Two very alert and energetic breeds, these animals are especially protective of children. Approaching strangers will likely receive an unpleasant greeting; Tervurens are inclined to attack unless commanded to desist. Both breeds are nevertheless quite intelligent, and respond well to obedience training. Adults range in size from two to two-and-a-half feet tall, and typically weigh between seventy-five and eighty pounds. They have squarish bodies, triangular faces, and fluffy tails. Their coats incline toward the long side, and require a solid half hour of brushing once a week. Sheepdogs are usually all black, while Tervurens have rich brown fur with black tips.

German Shepherds. The paragon of guard dogs is supremely intelligent and—unlike many dogs—actively enjoys training. Happiest when duty calls, German shepherds are often used for patrols, rescue missions, and search operations, and willingly serve as guides for physically challenged persons. They live for activity, and may become neurotic if forced to sit too long on the sidelines. Since German shepherds need to look up to their masters, timid or uncertain persons should consider another type of dog. On the other hand, with proper obedience training, shepherds are known for their commitment to children and other vulnerable individuals.

Loyal Dogs

Cats are congenial in their way, birds hold conversations, and horses certainly appear to have more sense than the majority of people; but for true companionship, no animal can rival a dog. Treated with love and respect, most dogs will respond attentively to their owners. Significant exceptions include those who suffered cruelty or neglect, were raised by nervous or timid owners, or were deprived of human contact altogether. Such animals may never fully trust people. Psychological abnormalities, though rare, may also render a dog hostile or suspicious.

Descriptions of the canine heart generally read like the Boy Scout creed. Yet devotion is often a function of individual temperament and genetic tendency. Certain breeds seem to thrive on human closeness, yearning to participate in all manner of dull or trivial pursuits. Some may love more quietly than others, but their loyalty is no less true. Among those distinguished for their passion for all things human are:

Keeshonden. Thought to have descended from Scandinavian sled dogs, keeshonden are compact animals with ravishingly thick fur and tightly curled, plumed tails. Their soft undercoat is either pale gray or cream-colored, while the bushy outer coat is typically a mix of gray and black. Extensive brushing is required twice a week to keep their fur glossy and free of tangles. Keeshonden have intelligent, foxlike faces and small, pointed ears; pale rings around their eyes look like spectacles. Gentle by nature, and quite glamorous in appearance, they make exceptional companions for people who don't necessarily fancy outdoor sports.

Lakeland Terriers. Enthusiasm is the hallmark of this breed. They cherish any activity that involves their owners—though, as terriers, they prefer energetic games to relaxing by the pool. Still, if loafing or puttering is your cup of tea, a Lakeland will happily oblige. Neglect is the one thing she can't abide. Clever and persistent, she will find ways to make herself noticed until you give her the attention she deserves. Such behavior is not to be confused with weakness or dependency. Though small in stature, Lakelands are courageous animals, and will fight other dogs if the mood strikes.

Scottish Deerhounds. Called "the most perfect creature" by Sir Walter Scott, the Scottish deerhound enjoyed the company of kings and assorted potentates for hundreds of years. Loyal, calm, and gentle, dogs of this breed possess the graceful build of greyhounds and the stamina typically associated with working dogs. Adults stand almost three feet tall, and weigh between 80 and 110 pounds. Their coat is wiry and usually blue, though they sport somewhat paler and silkier beards. A handsome addition to any throne room, Scottish deerhounds lend an air of elegance to all environments.

Loving Dogs

While many people enjoy simply knowing a devoted companion shares their lives, others crave more obvious demonstrations of affection. The difference here is mainly stylistic. For most dogs, the love felt for a master is simple, direct, and pure. Though the particular manner in which it finds expression may vary, the essence remains the same.

Nevertheless, certain people who are themselves outgoing naturally prefer the company of similarly ebullient companions. They want a dog who will bark happily every time the car pulls into the driveway, and leap all over them as they come through the door—licking, snuffling, and otherwise demonstrating feelings of transcendent bliss. It should be noted that dogs of this sort are not ideally suited for persons who have a strong attachment to clothing. Handsome sweaters and dark suits tend to collect dog hair rather easily, and ecstatic puppy claw marks can ruin a fine blouse. Those who desire a relationship of unadulterated mutual affection may wish to explore one of the following breeds.

Chihuahuas. Somewhat reserved around strangers, Chihuahuas frankly adore friends and family members. They are alert, intelligent, and extremely clean. Ideal for those who don't like going outside much, Chihuahuas are easily paper-trained. Owners, however, should not expect them to handle both indoor and outdoor bathroom privileges: A paper-trained pet remains paper-trained forever. The tiniest of breeds, adult Chihuahuas stand five inches tall at most, and weigh between two and four pounds. Their physical fragility does not suit them to outdoor activities, except for brief runs on warm days; nor can they withstand rough handling by small children. Chihuahuas enjoy nothing better than sitting on a lap, licking the hand that feeds them and kissing the face that tells them how adorable they are.

Golden Retrievers. Greeting cards and calendars are often graced with photographs of golden puppies, dressed in fancy clothes or simply staring wistfully at the camera. Even as adults, golden retrievers lose none of the happy nature that indulges such undignified treatment. Though it's possible to find a grumpy or aggressive golden, by and large the breed deserves its reputation as an ideal family pet. Goldens equally enjoy staring quietly at their owners with rapt adoration or racing after a stick. They love jogging, swimming, hiking, watching television, and resting their muzzles in a warm lap. They are notoriously attractive animals, large and powerfully built, with smiling faces, rich brown eyes, and thick coats of butterscotch-colored fur. Though content to live in a city apartment, they do need a good deal of exercise.

Vizslas. Tall, lean, and graceful, these handsome sporting dogs are demonstrably affectionate with their families, though somewhat wary of strangers. The breed originated in Hungary, and the extraordinarily deep bond between vizslas and their owners can be affirmed by the fact that Hungarians insisted on taking their dogs with them when they fled their native land in large numbers during World War II. Vizslas are pointers, physically compact, with broad chests and long, square muzzles. They have short, smooth coats that range in color from sandy yellow to deep gold. Highly active, they don't adapt well to city life, and may not enjoy suburban living. They are best suited to the country.

Yorkshire Terriers. Yorkies respond well to pampering; in fact, they insist on it. Yet they are apt to return every affectionate gesture four times over. Yorkshire terriers thus make the perfect pet for people who want to spend a lot of time coddling someone and being coddled in return. They like to talk, and tend to have an opinion about everything—especially about being left behind. They expect to accompany their owners everywhere, and are fortunately small enough to accommodate. Yorkies are usually only six or seven inches tall, and their average weight hovers around four pounds. They have long, silky coats, which require daily brushing. Remarkably intelligent, they're easy to train, and likely to manipulate their owners.

Quiet Dogs

Those who desire a calm, undemanding companion need not despair of finding a dog who shares their taste for serenity. A number of breeds have been specifically developed for their gentle, reserved temperaments. These animals are neither dull nor unaffectionate. They simply choose to express themselves discreetly.

Placid dogs make fine companions for people who prefer a tranquil atmosphere. They adapt well to tidy homes and can usually be counted on to respect fine furnishings and collector's items. Individuals who are either physically or temperamentally incapable of caring for an energetic animal will find a lovely friend in a quiet, easygoing dog. Even if your situation doesn't absolutely cry out for a docile companion, you may nevertheless feel drawn to a pet like one of the breeds described below.

Basenjis. Those who find the typical canine voice a bit irritating will be glad to know that basenjis don't bark. Quiet as a rule, they occasionally express themselves with a pleasant-sounding chuckle or mellow yodeling sound. They are swift, lean dogs, of medium height and proud bearing. Their coats are short and silky, easy to groom, though inadequate for cold weather; dog blankets and draft-free beds are recommended. They shed very little, and give off virtually no odor—a decided advantage for people suffering from allergies. Basenjis may be chestnut-colored, black, or black and tan, with white markings on the chest, feet, legs, and the tip of their tightly curled tails.

Bouvier des Flandres. A very docile animal, the Bouvier des Flandres may appear aloof even around people he knows quite well. Don't be fooled by his apparent indifference, however. As a herding dog, he is keenly aware of his environment; he's simply not given to showing off. The breed is large and shaggy. Adults grow to about two-and-a-half feet or more, and weigh between eighty and ninety-five pounds. They have thick, rumpled coats, ranging from pale brown to black; a full beard and mustache complete the rugged effect. Too gentle for a guard dog, the Bouvier nevertheless has excellent territorial instincts, making him a good watchdog and a reliable baby-sitter. He likes to take long, rambling walks, and if this habit is daily indulged, he can adapt quite well to an urban setting.

English Setters. English setters tend to be less animated than other sporting dogs. They have excellent manners, perhaps because the breed originated in Renaissance Spain—a country noted for severe morals. Quietly aristocratic in the home, English setters are fond of children and other pets. They do, however, need a great deal of exercise, and should therefore only be considered by people with the time and stamina to oblige them. Standing roughly two feet tall and weighing approximately sixty-five to seventy pounds, English setters have moderately long, silken coats, plumed tails, and feathery chests. They range in color from solid black, tan, or white, to flecks of these colors on a solid background.

Italian Greyhounds. A miniature version of their racing cousins, Italian greyhounds are sleek, graceful little animals with refined temperaments. They are not overtly fond of handling or sitting on laps, preferring to pose comfortably on an elegant pillow or low chair near their owners. They are also extremely intelligent, and so sensitive to the moods of their owners that a harsh word is often the only reprimand they need. Adults grow to only fifteen inches tall, and weigh between five and eight pounds. Unlike most toy breeds, Italian greyhounds never stoop to whining or manipulation. In all situations, they remain elegant and serene.

Friendly Dogs

Somewhere between the demonstrative breeds and more reserved types are dogs known primarily for their sociable natures. These are the charmers of the canine kingdom, outgoing and easy to live with. As likely to wag their tails at a nighttime prowler as at an Avon lady, many in this category do not make very competent watchdogs. They do, however, function well in areas populated with children and friendly neighbors. People who entertain frequently will see the advantage of adopting a sociable dog. Few events can spoil a luncheon or birthday party as quickly as a lusty bite on the ankle, or a fit of loud, angry barking.

A friendly dog is pleasant to greet at the end of the day. Tired owners need not feel guilty if they can't work up the same enthusiasm as a pet who has been pacing around the house all day, waiting for the sound of the key in the door. Nor are they likely to feel rejected by one who simply gives a quick sniff before settling down again in front of the fireplace. Friendly dogs, such as those described below, enjoy being around people, but they don't depend on constant reassurance. They know you'll come around when you're ready.

Beagles. Small and good-natured, beagles are among the easiest dogs to steal. Matters are not helped by this breed's miraculous ability to work free of collars and leashes and roam the neighborhood. Owners are therefore advised to ask their veterinarians about tattooing their pet's ears. The popularity of beagles in recent decades has resulted in a certain weakening of bloodlines, resulting in irritable or high-strung puppies. However, when adopted from a reputable breeder, beagles make fine family pets. They love visitors and children, require only moderate exercise, and prefer a light massage to brushing or combing. Beagles have a tendency to howl; and though many do overcome the habit through training, not all of them are capable of doing so.

Brittanies. A sporting breed, Brittanies are active, intelligent, and extremely confident. They love to work, but don't suffer an overwhelming anxiety to please. Responsive to training, they tend to look up to their owners, in much the same way children in films and television of an earlier era regarded their fathers: with affection tempered by respect. You may recognize Brittanies from tapestries and paintings that grace the walls of hunting lodges and so forth. Their short, wavy coats are predominantly white, with brown- or liver-colored patches. Their ears hang close to their heads, and their noses are pink or light beige. Like most hunting dogs, they must follow a daily program of vigorous exercise.

Norfolk Terriers and Norwich Terriers. For sheer charisma, no other breed can match these animals. They are alert, inquisitive, and outgoing; and though not desperate to please, they enjoy ambling up to casual acquaintances and performing some trick or other to elicit gasps of admiration. Both breeds adapt beautifully to any environment, equally at home perched on an ottoman or chasing rats around the family barn. Both measure only ten inches tall and weigh close to ten pounds. Coats are wiry, dense, and moderately long; they may be red, wheat-colored, black and tan, or gray. Ears mark the difference between the breeds. Norwich terriers have sharp, erect ears, while those of a Norfolk are round and droop close to the cheeks.

Intelligent Dogs

People tend to boast about their dogs in much the same way they brag about their children. They're all beautiful, sweet, kind, funny, and endearing, and they're all budding geniuses. Once their progeny reach a certain age, however, many parents wax somewhat less enthusiastic. Curiously, dog owners rarely cease to rave about their dogs.

Occasionally an owner may slip, and grumble to a friend or neighbor about the latest calamity their clumsy pet has wreaked upon the household. Sometimes, too, a visitor may witness an unfortunate incident on the living room carpet or an embarrassing failure to comprehend a simple command. Such glimpses behind the facade of canine perfection, though rare, are nonetheless illuminating. A perceptive individual will no doubt deduce a certain weakness in the mythology widely circulated by dog owners. Simply put, not all dogs are smart.

Conversely, some dogs are very smart. With very little effort, they learn to heel, fetch, sit, stand, bark, not bark, stay off the couch, and grab the leash. More advanced students learn the difference between red lights and green lights, subtle methods of sniffing out contraband, or the etiquette of pulling wayward skiers from a snowbank. Serious professionals can be taught to execute a variety of complicated tasks under glaring klieg lights, while the cameras roll. Perhaps the most cunning of all merely pretend to be dim, thereby avoiding long hours of grueling training.

Adopting a highly intelligent dog simplifies housebreaking, training, and other assorted obligations. Owners must beware, though, that smart dogs are apt to pick up a few skills on their own time. Opening doors, stealthily plucking forbidden morsels from the garbage, slithering out of collars, and similar maneuvers can provoke all manner of unpleasant repercussions. Improprieties must be firmly discouraged. Still, a clever dog usually makes life enjoyable and pleasant for her owner, and any of the following breeds may be reliably and loudly praised for their mental abilities.

Affenpinschers. Don't be taken in by their sweet, comical faces: This toy breed is smart, and knows it. Though affenpinschers don't require much exercise, they derive immense satisfaction from amusing their owners with tricks and games. In return, of course, they expect a good deal of praise and mounds of treats.

Avoid overfeeding these little manipulators; adult affenpinschers should weigh no more than seven or eight pounds. They look like terriers, with short, wiry coats, eager expressions, and prominent tufts on the face and head. Fiercely devoted to people they know, yet highly suspicious of strangers, affenpinschers make surprisingly good watchdogs.

Border Collies. Bred for intelligence and ability, border collies are without a doubt one of the smartest breeds around. They have become quite popular in Hollywood in recent years, demonstrating not only an uncanny ability to learn new skills faster than most actors, but a far superior physical endurance as well. These superb animals were bred to herd sheep, a job that requires sound judgment and constant exertion. Unfortunately, the combination of fierce intelligence and inexhaustible energy is probably too much for the ordinary dog owner. A border collie must be challenged, physically and mentally. If you don't have any sheep to herd, you'll have to devise other chores for him; otherwise, he'll become extremely destructive.

The herding instinct runs very deep in these dogs. They will literally attempt to herd anything that moves, whether it's livestock, birds, other dogs, cats, children, lights, or running water. This may be amusing at first glance; to a child, however, the experience is likely to be terrifying. Adults, meanwhile, can easily become annoyed by the constant bid for attention. Border collies require human participation in their exercise programs. They do not consider being left to run around in a fenced area as a form of exercise. If you do not have the time or energy to devote to this remarkable breed, there are better choices available.

Poodles. Often dismissed as spoiled, petty creatures, poodles are among the cleverest canines available. Many of the misconceptions surrounding this breed stem from the belief that it originated in France as the darling of spoiled aristocratic ladies. Although the breed enjoys great popularity there, its origins lie more properly in Germany and Russia. The poodle originally served as a retriever, fetching game from water; its shaved coat had less to do with fashion than with function, enhancing the dog's ability to swim. Both the standard and miniature versions of this breed are hardy, agile animals, quick to learn and willing to work hard for their supper. Like any dog, they can be spoiled by too much fussing, while rhinestone collars and silly names compound the problem. Standard sizes range from twenty-two to twenty-six inches tall; miniatures between ten and fifteen inches. Toy poodles, though more fragile than their relations, are no less intelligent. Adults of this variety are usually no more than ten inches tall.

Welsh Terriers. This breed of terrier tends to be less aggressive than most. Contentious tendencies were carefully bred out of the line, allowing a strong commitment to work and a fine instinct for hunting to dominate. Welsh terriers are sensible and curious, and unusually sensitive to shifts in their owners' moods. They enjoy companionship, but can entertain themselves for considerable periods. Since fetching is their favorite sport, owners should indulge them regularly or their clever little minds will devise more destructive games. Long walks on a leash also satisfy their need for stimulation. Welsh terriers have dense and wiry coats, which require brushing three times a week. A bath once a month is also recommended. Adults are typically thirteen to fifteen inches tall, and weigh about twenty pounds.

Dogs Who Like Children

No breeder can guarantee that a certain breed will or will not get along well with children. Dogs and children are both unpredictable. It's virtually impossible to say with absolute certainty what lurks behind their sweet faces. Bear in mind that all dogs are descended from wolves. Their aggressive and defensive instincts run very deep, and their bodies have been designed to hunt and kill. Their jaws can exert tremendous pressure—a thousand pounds per square inch in the case of German shepherds—and can therefore inflict tremendous pain and damage. *Consequently, all early encounters between dogs and children must be closely supervised.*

Unfortunately, two of the breeds most noted for their affectionate natures—beagles and cocker spaniels—have been routinely bred by careless or unscrupulous persons. As a result, many of these dogs can be nervous, hostile, and extremely intolerant of children. Spaniels in particular seem to have an unpredictable vicious streak. *If you intend to bring a dog of either breed into a home with children, it is absolutely essential to acquire the animal from an unimpeachable source.* Dalmatians, no matter how well-bred, tend to be high-strung animals, with a low tolerance for shrill voices and energetic behavior. They must be introduced to children early on or their nervous temperaments will get the better of them. Finally, most toys don't like the rough sort of love very small children are apt to show them.

On the other hand, terriers, golden retrievers, and several of the guard dog breeds seem to adapt fairly readily to children. Individual character and prior history can influence any dog in peculiar ways, of course, so you must supervise all early inter- actions. Yet once a bond has been established, the relationship between child and dog is often powerful and touching; happy memories will likely warm both partners even after years of sep- aration. Those wishing to provide such a gift to their children may want to consider one of the following breeds.

Collies. Unfortunately, a popular television series that shall re- main nameless has burdened collies with a reputation for initiative they don't necessarily deserve. Though reasonably smart and easy to train, most examples of this breed are not likely to foil the plans of international jewel thieves, or run twenty miles through the woods to tell a ranger about a little boy stuck in a tree. They are far more apt to stop along the way and socialize with the first group of picnickers they see, while the jewel thieves escape and little Timmy cries himself hoarse in the tree. Still, many people find it hard to resist admiring members of this handsome, gre- garious breed. Children especially adore collies, and—perhaps owing to a similarly trusting and simple nature—collies adore children to the same degree.

Gordon Setters. Sturdy, beautiful, and kind, Gordon setters have earned a reputation for their affection toward children. Their strong commitment to protect their families may incline them to- ward possessiveness, and they won't take kindly to advances made by other dogs. Firm training is required to curb this jealous streak; however, because they live to please their owners, most Gordons will quickly comply. They are active, energetic animals, and deserve long periods of exercise. Of medium height and build, they have soft, black coats with rich brown markings and some feathering around their ears, chest, legs, and tails. Weekly brushing will keep them looking trim and glossy.

Labrador Retrievers. Though less sparkling in appearance than their golden cousins, Labradors are no less affectionate and eager to please. Largely intelligent animals, Labradors adapt exception- ally to all variety of households. They adore children and get along handsomely with other pets, and though apt to insert them- selves into any situation, they aren't particularly nosy. They just like to say hello every five minutes or so and find out if you still love them. Labradors have short, dense coats—usually either chocolate, yellow, or black—and are therefore easy to groom. As with all sporting dogs, they need a good workout every day.

Dogs Who Like Cities

Most dogs frankly prefer a suburban or rural setting. Room to wander, a variety of scents, and a bit of grass to roll in or to chew when it becomes necessary to throw up make a dog's life far more pleasant than the image usually associated with the phrase. Urban environments, on the other hand, offer far too much stimulus and far too little space for the majority of canines. Giant animals, like Newfoundlands, Saint Bernards, and Great Danes, can feel cramped even in moderately large apartments; deprived of the chance to run, most sporting dogs grow anxious and irritable; even the most docile herding dog is apt to go mad investigating the same boring territory day after day.

While it would be unfair to suggest that urbanites forgo the pleasure of a dog's company, it is equally shortsighted to trap a dog in a setting she finds uniquely hostile. Fortunately, toys and terriers adapt quite easily to life in the big city, although terriers require longer periods of exercise or walking. Even the larger terrier breeds, such as Airedales, Irish, Kerry blues, Lakelands, and wirehaired foxes, are physically compact enough to live in an apartment without feeling as though they're carrying out a prison term.

Still, toys generally require more pampering than some people are willing to give; and while undoubtedly charming, attractive, and alert, they don't offer the kind of security many apartment dwellers seek. Terriers, meanwhile, do not appeal to everyone. Certain people find them too aggressive, and their wiry coats need more attention than some people are willing to give. Should you find yourself in a dilemma of this sort, a number of sturdy breeds have proven themselves willing and able to enjoy life in a glittering metropolis.

French Bulldogs. Clean, quiet, and easygoing, French bulldogs thrive best in one-on-one relationships. Among families, they tend to compete for attention with children and other pets. They learn easily, and though occasionally stubborn, with firm training and a good deal of affection they are remarkably easy to keep. A bracing rubdown with a rough cloth is all the grooming care they

need, while a brisk walk twice a day satisfies their exercise requirements. Registries recognize two classes of French bulldog:
smaller fellows under twenty-two pounds, and larger ones,
twenty-two to twenty-eight pounds. Both categories stand around
a foot tall, with broad chests and narrow hind ends. The breed is
notable for a large, square head and domed forehead, batlike ears,
and square lower jaws. Because their front legs are usually shorter
than the back legs, French bulldogs tend to carry themselves like
tiny, overzealous weight lifters.

Welsh Corgis. Neither the Cardigan nor the Pembroke variety
seem to know they're small dogs. Alert, courageous, and unusually attentive to small sounds and strange scents, both breeds
make excellent watchdogs. Their craving for affection far exceeds
their stature, but most people find it hard to deny them love and
attention. Corgis have an instinct for play, and their smiling faces
are a welcome sight at any time of day. They do well in pairs,
capable of amusing each other for long periods when no one else
is around. Adults rarely grow larger than a foot tall, though the
average length may exceed three feet. Originally bred for herding,
they love to run and should be taken out twice a day on a long
leash. Cardigans have thick, stiff coats of medium length, bushy
tails, and somewhat blunted muzzles. Pembrokes have straighter,
smoother coats, longer muzzles, and no tail. While a variety of
colors are seen in both breeds, Pembrokes are more inclined to
wear paler coats than their cousins.

Cavalier King Charles Spaniels. Descended from the toy spaniels of Europe, the cavalier King Charles was extremely popular
among the British aristocracy and a favorite subject of court painters. These lovely animals have long silky coats, feathered along
the ears, legs, tail, and feet. On average, they stand between
twelve and thirteen inches tall and weigh between twelve and
eighteen pounds.

Cavaliers can be quite enjoyable to train, since they're usually
smart and eager to please. They are inclined to roam, however.
If you have a yard, you'll need to inspect every inch of fence.
Cavaliers can squeeze through amazingly small cracks and gaps,
and seem to have an instinct for finding them. It's especially un-
wise to let a Cavalier wander away while still on a leash, since
more than one case of accidental hanging has been recorded.

Elegant, confident, and friendly, Cavaliers combine the best
traits of both the toy and the sporting variety. They enjoy a bit

of exercise, but as befits their noble heritage, they practice moderation in all things. Unlike other varieties of spaniel, Cavaliers typically get along very nicely with children. In fact, they appear to be blessed with a very stable temperament—which, together with their distinctly regal appearance, makes the Cavalier an ideal pet for just about any household.

Dogs with Distinction

Like intelligence, appearance is a touchy subject among dog owners. Most consider their dogs beautiful, and they have every right to think so. Nature has not stinted in fashioning her canine children—though, like many artists, she occasionally rises to new heights of miraculous inspiration. Whether mere mortals judge their looks beautiful or upsetting, dogs of distinction command attention wherever they go.

Afghan Hounds. Tall and exceptionally slim, Afghans are high-fashion animals. They have tapering muzzles, slender hips, and graceful necks. Their bodies are covered with very long, silky hair, except around the face and saddle. Their tails look like thin lengths of rope. Originally bred to hunt leopards and gazelles, Afghans can reach speeds of up to twenty-eight miles an hour, so exercise should include at least one free run a day, in addition to a long walk on a leash. Afghans are wary of strangers, and should therefore be socialized widely from an early age to overcome their shyness.

Bedlington Terriers. For anyone with a yen for the truly bizarre, Bedlington terriers may be the answer. Slender and arched like a greyhound, Bedlingtons are covered with kinky, short fur, which is usually trimmed in an even line from the top of the head to the tip of the nose. Their long, droopy ears are shaved clean except for a pompom at the tip. As a result, Bedlingtons look like a mischievous experiment with dogs and lambs. Actually, their heritage is more likely a mix of terrier and small hound. They are very fast and somewhat stubborn, and should only be exercised off-leash in a securely enclosed area.

Bullmastiffs. Adults of this giant breed cannot help but inspire awe in the beholder. Well over two feet tall and weighing more than 130 pounds, bullmastiffs have broad, wrinkled muzzles and a pronounced underbite. Their short, thick coats are typically red or golden brown, with black markings across the face. Like an ocean liner pulling into port, the bullmastiff carries itself majestically and a bit ponderously, though when roused, he can move with deadly swiftness. This is not a breed for casual owners. Obedience training is absolutely mandatory; undisciplined, these powerful dogs pose a threat to owners and strangers alike.

Komondors. This unusual breed can trace its origins back more than one thousand years to the broad mountains of Hungary, where its forebears protected flocks from ravaging wolves, bears, and other predators. Like most herd dogs, komondors needed a tough coat to withstand rough weather and potentially deadly assaults, and nature provided an extraordinary solution. The komondor's body is covered with white woolly cords that hang close to the ground. To the casual observer, a komondor appears to have been drenched in glue and set loose in a yarn factory. Professional grooming advice should be sought to care for this breed. Komondors can be stubborn and aggressive, so obedience training is essential. Grooming, moreover, will consume a good deal of time every day.

BREED CHARTS

The following charts are offered as an aid to choosing the right dog for your needs. Several categories have been incorporated, including breed group, temperament, suitability for urban life, grooming needs, and activity level.

This summary is by no means exhaustive. For a thorough understanding of a particular breed, you'll want to consult a few of the sources mentioned in Chapter Two. Each person you speak with and each publication you read will probably offer a slightly different perspective. Taking the time to consult several different sources should help you to develop a fairly well-rounded understanding of the breed in question. Among the points you'll want to consider are:

- Origins of the breed
- Recent history (including possible overbreeding or popularity)
- Temperament
- Exercise needs
- Suitability to rural, suburban, or urban setting
- Ease of training

- Grooming needs
- Breed-related medical problems

You'll also want to explore matters relating to your personal situation, such as the breed's sociability, attitude toward children, and so forth.

BREED	BODY TYPE	TEMPERAMENT	EXERCISE NEEDS	COAT	SUITABILITY
Sporting Dogs					
Brittany	M	Loyal, Intelligent	Heavy	Short	C, P, W
Pointer	L	Loyal, Intelligent	Heavy	Short	
German Shorthaired Pointer	L	Loyal, Intelligent	Heavy	Short	
German Wirehaired Pointer	L	Loyal	Heavy	Wiry	W
Chesapeake Bay Retriever	L	Loyal, Friendly, Intelligent	Heavy	Short	C, W
Curly-Coated Retriever	L	Loyal, Loving, Intelligent	Heavy	Curly	C, W
Flat-Coated Retriever	L	Loyal, Loving, Intelligent	Heavy	Short	C, P
Golden Retriever	L	Loyal, Loving, Friendly, Intelligent	Heavy	Dense	C, P, U
Labrador Retriever	L	Loyal, Loving, Friendly	Heavy	Curly	C, P, U

BREED	BODY TYPE	TEMPERAMENT	EXERCISE NEEDS	COAT	SUITABILITY
English Setter	L	Loyal, Loving, Quiet	Heavy	Long	C, P
Gordon Setter	L	Loyal, Loving, Intelligent	Heavy	Short	C, W, G
Irish Setter	L	Loyal, Loving, Friendly, Intelligent	Heavy	Long	C, P
American Water Spaniel	L	Loyal, Loving, Friendly, Intelligent	Heavy	Curly	C, P, W
Clumber Spaniel	M	Loyal, Quiet	Moderate	Dense, unusual	C, W
Cocker Spaniel	S	Loving, Friendly, Intelligent	Moderate	Long	U
English Cocker Spaniel	S	Loyal, Friendly, Intelligent	Moderate	Long	C
English Springer Spaniel	S	Loyal, Friendly, Intelligent	Moderate	Short	C, U
Field Spaniel	S	Loyal, Quiet, Intelligent	Heavy	Long	C, P, W
Irish Water Spaniel	M	Loyal, Intelligent	Heavy	Curly	W, G

Key: C–Children, P–Other pets, U–Urban life, W–Watchdog, G–Guard dog

BREED	BODY TYPE	TEMPERAMENT	EXERCISE NEEDS	COAT	SUITABILITY
Sussex Spaniel	M	Loyal, Loving, Quiet	Moderate	Short	C, U, W, G
Welch Springer Spaniel	M	Loyal, Quiet, Intelligent	Heavy	Short	C, W, G
Vizsla	L	Loving, Quiet, Intelligent	Heavy	Short	C, W, G
Weimaraner	L	Loyal, Intelligent	Heavy	Short	W
Wirehaired Pointing Griffon	S	Loyal, Quiet, Intelligent	Heavy	Wiry	W
Hounds					
Afghan	L	Loving, Quiet	Heavy	Long	W
Basenji	M	Loyal, Loving, Quiet, Intelligent	Moderate	Short	
Basset	M	Loyal, Loving, Quiet, Friendly	Moderate	Short	C, U

BREED	BODY TYPE	TEMPERAMENT	EXERCISE NEEDS	COAT	SUITABILITY
Beagle	S	Loyal, Loving, Friendly, Intelligent	Moderate	Short	C, P, U, W
Black-and-Tan Coonhound	M	Loyal, Quiet, Friendly, Intelligent	Heavy	Short	W
English Coonhound	M	Loyal, Friendly, Intelligent	Heavy	Short	C, W
Redbone Coonhound	M	Loyal, Friendly, Intelligent	Heavy	Short	C, P, W
Bloodhound	Giant	Loyal, Friendly, Intelligent	Heavy	Short	C, P, W
Borzoi	Giant	Loyal, Loving, Friendly	Moderate	Unusual	C
Dachshund[1]	S	Loyal, Loving, Friendly, Intelligent	Minimal	Long, wiry, or short	C, P, U
American Foxhound	M	Loyal, Loving, Quiet, Intelligent	Heavy	Short	C, W, G

[1]Three different coat types: longhaired, wirehaired, and shorthaired

Key: C-Children, P-Other pets, U-Urban life, W-Watchdog, G-Guard dog

BREED	BODY TYPE	TEMPERAMENT	EXERCISE NEEDS	COAT	SUITABILITY
English Foxhound	M	Loyal, Loving, Friendly,	Heavy	Short	W
Greyhound	L	Loyal, Quiet, Intelligent	Heavy	Short	W
Harrier	M	Loyal, Quiet, Friendly, Intelligent	Heavy	Short	C, W
Ibizan Hound	L	Loyal, Quiet, Friendly, Intelligent	Heavy	Short	C, W
Irish Wolfhound	Giant	Loving, Quiet, Friendly	Moderate	Wiry	C
Norwegian Elkhound	M	Loyal, Loving	Moderate	Dense	C, U, W, G
Otter Hound	L	Loyal, Loving, Friendly	Heavy	Dense	C, W, G
Pharaoh Hound	M	Loyal, Loving, Intelligent	Heavy	Short	C, W

BREED	BODY TYPE	TEMPERAMENT	EXERCISE NEEDS	COAT	SUITABILITY
Plott Hound	M	Loyal, Friendly	Heavy	Short	C, W, G
Rhodesian Ridgeback	L	Loving, Intelligent	Heavy	Short, unusual	W
Saluki[1]	L	Loyal, Loving, Quiet	Heavy	Long or short	C, W
Scottish Deerhound	Giant	Loyal, Loving, Quiet	Heavy	Wiry	C
Whippet	M	Loyal, Loving, Friendly, Intelligent	Heavy	Short	C, U, W
Working Dogs					
Akita	Giant	Loyal, Loving, Intelligent	Heavy	Dense	W, G
Alaskan Malamute	L	Loyal, Loving, Friendly	Moderate	Dense	C, W

[1] Two different coat types: long- and shorthaired

Key: C–Children, P–Other pets, U–Urban life, W–Watchdog, G–Guard dog

BREED	BODY TYPE	TEMPERAMENT	EXERCISE NEEDS	COAT	SUITABILITY
American Eskimo[1]	S/M	Loving, Friendly, Intelligent	Moderate	Dense	C, U, W
Bernese Mountain Dog	L	Loyal, Quiet, Intelligent	Moderate	Dense	C, W, G
Boxer	M	Loving, Friendly, Intelligent	Heavy	Short	C, U, W, G
Bullmastiff	Giant	Loyal, Intelligent	Moderate	Short	W, G
Doberman Pinscher	L	Loyal, Intelligent	Heavy	Short	W, G
Giant Schnauzer	L	Loyal, Loving, Intelligent	Moderate	Dense	C, W
Great Dane	Giant	Loyal, Loving, Friendly, Intelligent	Heavy	Short	C, W, G
Great Pyrenees	Giant	Loyal, Loving, Quiet	Heavy	Dense	W
Komondor	L	Loyal, Loving	Heavy/Moderate	Long, unusual	W

[1] Two different sizes: standard and miniature

BREED	BODY TYPE	TEMPERAMENT	EXERCISE NEEDS	COAT	SUITABILITY
Kuvasz	Giant	Loyal, Friendly, Intelligent	Moderate	Dense	C, W, G
Mastiff	Giant	Loyal, Friendly	Minimal	Short	W, G
Newfoundland	Giant	Loving, Friendly, Intelligent	Heavy	Dense	C, P, W
Portuguese Water Dog	M	Friendly, Intelligent	Moderate	Curly	C
Rottweiler	L	Loyal, Intelligent	Heavy	Short	W, G
Saint Bernard	Giant	Loving, Quiet, Friendly, Intelligent	Moderate	Dense	C, W
Samoyed	M	Loving, Friendly, Intelligent	Moderate	Dense	C, P, W
Siberian Husky	M	Loyal, Loving, Intelligent	Heavy	Dense	C, G
Standard Schnauzer	M	Loving, Friendly, Intelligent	Moderate	Wiry	C, W

Key: C–Children, P–Other pets, U–Urban life, W–Watchdog, G–Guard dog

BREED	BODY TYPE	TEMPERAMENT	EXERCISE NEEDS	COAT	SUITABILITY
Terriers					
Airedale	M	Loyal, Loving, Friendly	Moderate	Wiry	C, U, W
American Staffordshire	M	Loyal, Loving, Intelligent	Heavy	Short	U, W, G
Australian	S	Loyal, Friendly, Intelligent	Moderate	Dense	C, P, U, W
Bedlington	M	Loyal, Friendly	Heavy	Curly	C, U, W
Border	S	Loyal, Loving, Intelligent	Moderate	Wiry, unusual	C, P, U, W
Bull	M	Loyal, Loving, Intelligent	Moderate	Short	C, U, W
Cairn	S	Loyal, Loving, Friendly	Moderate	Wiry	C, P, U, W
Dandie Dinmont	S	Loyal, Loving, Quiet	Moderate	Curly, unusual	U, W
Irish	M	Loyal, Loving, Intelligent	Moderate	Dense, wiry	C, U, W, G

BREED	BODY TYPE	TEMPERAMENT	EXERCISE NEEDS	COAT	SUITABILITY
Kerry Blue	M	Loyal, Loving, Intelligent	Moderate	Dense, curly	C, U, W, G
Lakeland	S	Loyal, Loving, Friendly	Moderate	Dense, wiry	C, U, W
Manchester	S	Loyal, Loving, Intelligent	Moderate	Short	C, U, W, G
Miniature Schnauzer	S	Loyal, Loving, Intelligent	Moderate	Dense, wiry	C, U, W
Norfolk	S	Loving, Friendly, Intelligent	Minimal	Wiry	C, U, W
Norwich	S	Loving, Friendly, Intelligent	Minimal	Wiry	C, U, W
Scottish	S	Loyal, Loving, Intelligent	Minimal	Wiry	U, W
Sealyham	S	Loyal, Loving, Friendly	Moderate	Long, wiry	C, U, W

Key: C–Children, P–Other pets, U–Urban life, W–Watchdog, G–Guard dog

BREED	BODY TYPE	TEMPERAMENT	EXERCISE NEEDS	COAT	SUITABILITY
Skye	S	Loyal, Loving, Intelligent	Moderate	Long	C, U, W
Smooth Fox	S	Loving, Friendly	Heavy	Short	C, U, W
Staffordshire Bull	M	Loyal, Loving, Friendly	Moderate	Short	C, U, W, G
Welsh	M	Loyal, Quiet, Intelligent	Moderate	Wiry	C, U, W
West Highland White	S	Loving, Friendly	Moderate	Dense, wiry	C, P, U, W
Wheaten	M	Loyal, Friendly, Intelligent	Moderate	Long, unusual	C, P, U, W
Wire Fox	M	Loyal, Friendly, Intelligent	Moderate	Wiry, unusual	C, U, W
Toys					
Affenpinscher	S	Loving, Intelligent	Minimal	Wiry	P, U, W
Brussels Griffon	S	Loving, Friendly, Intelligent	Minimal	Wiry	P, U, W

BREED	BODY TYPE	TEMPERAMENT	EXERCISE NEEDS	COAT	SUITABILITY
Chihuahua	S	Loyal, Loving, Intelligent	Minimal	Short	P, U, W
English Toy Spaniel	S	Loving, Friendly	Minimal	Long	C, U, W
Italian Greyhound	S	Loving, Quiet, Intelligent	Minimal	Short	U
Japanese Chin	S	Loyal, Loving, Friendly, Intelligent	Minimal	Long	U
Maltese	S	Loving, Friendly, Intelligent	Minimal	Long	U, W
Miniature Pinscher	S	Loyal, Friendly, Intelligent	Moderate	Short	C, U, W
Papillon	S	Loving, Friendly, Intelligent	Minimal	Long	C, P, U
Pekingese	S	Loyal, Loving, Intelligent	Minimal	Long	U, W

Key: C–Children, P–Other pets, U–Urban life, W–Watchdog, G–Guard dog

BREED	BODY TYPE	TEMPERAMENT	EXERCISE NEEDS	COAT	SUITABILITY
Pomeranian	S	Friendly	Minimal	Long, dense, unusual	U, W
Pug	S	Loyal, Loving, Friendly	Minimal	Short	C, P, U
Shih Tzu	S	Loyal, Loving, Friendly, Intelligent	Minimal	Long, dense	C, U
Silky Terrier	S	Loving, Intelligent	Minimal	Long	U, W
Toy Fox Terrier	S	Loyal, Loving, Friendly, Intelligent	Moderate	Short	U, W
Toy Manchester Terrier	S	Loving, Friendly, Intelligent	Moderate	Short	U, W
Yorkshire Terrier	S	Loyal, Loving, Friendly, Intelligent	Minimal	Long	C, P, U, W
Nonsporting Dogs					
Bichon Frise	S	Loving, Friendly, Intelligent	Minimal	Dense, curly, unusual	C, P, U

BREED	BODY TYPE	TEMPERAMENT	EXERCISE NEEDS	COAT	SUITABILITY
Boston Terrier	S	Loyal, Loving, Friendly, Intelligent	Moderate	Short	C, P, U, W
Bulldog	M	Loyal, Quiet, Friendly	Minimal	Short	C, U, W
Chow Chow	M	Loyal, Intelligent	Moderate	Long, dense	W, G
Dalmatian	M	Loyal, Intelligent	Heavy	Short, unusual	W, G
French Bulldog	S	Loyal, Loving	Minimal	Short	U, W
Keeshond	M	Loyal, Loving, Friendly, Intelligent	Moderate	Long, dense	C, U, W
Lhasa Apso	S	Loyal, Loving	Moderate	Long, unusual	U
Poodle[1]	M, S	Loyal, Friendly, Intelligent	Heavy/Moderate	Curly	U, W
Schipperke	S	Loyal, Loving, Intelligent	Moderate	Long, curly	C, U, W, G
Tibetan Spaniel	S	Loving, Friendly, Intelligent	Heavy	Long	U, W

[1] Available in three sizes: standard, miniature, and toy

Key: C–Children, P–Other pets, U–Urban life, W–Watchdog, G–Guard dog

BREED	BODY TYPE	TEMPERAMENT	EXERCISE NEEDS	COAT	SUITABILITY
Tibetan Terrier	S	Loyal, Friendly, Intelligent	Moderate	Long, dense	C, P, U, W
Herd Dogs					
Australian Cattle Dog	M	Loyal, Intelligent	Heavy	Short	W, G
Australian Shepherd	M	Loyal, Loving, Intelligent	Heavy	Long, dense	C, W, G
Bearded Collie	M	Loyal, Loving, Friendly	Heavy	Long, dense	C, P, U, W
Belgian Malinois	L	Loyal, Loving, Intelligent	Heavy	Dense, short	C, W, G
Belgian Sheepdog	L	Loyal, Loving, Intelligent	Heavy	Long	C, W, G
Belgian Tervuren	L	Loyal, Loving, Friendly, Intelligent	Heavy	Long	C, W, G
Border Collie	L	Loyal, Quiet, Intelligent	Heavy	Dense	C, W, G
Bouvier des Flandres	L	Loyal, Loving, Quiet	Heavy	Dense, wiry	C

BREED	BODY TYPE	TEMPERAMENT	EXERCISE NEEDS	COAT	SUITABILITY
Briard	L	Loyal, Intelligent	Moderate	Long, wiry	W, G
Collie	L	Loyal, Loving, Friendly, Intelligent	Heavy	Long, dense	C, P U, W
English Shepherd	M	Loyal, Loving, Intelligent	Heavy	Dense	W, G
German Shepherd	L	Loyal, Loving, Intelligent.	Heavy	Short	C, P, U, W, G
Old English Sheepdog	L	Loyal, Loving, Friendly	Heavy	Long, dense	P, W
Puli	S	Loyal, Loving	Heavy	Long, unusual	C, W
Shetland Sheepdog	S	Loyal, Loving, Friendly	Moderate	Long	C, P, U, W
Welsh Corgi	S	Loyal, Loving, Friendly, Intelligent	Moderate	Short	C, P, U, W

Key: C–Children, P–Other pets, U–Urban life, W–Watchdog, G–Guard dog

Chapter 4

From House to Home

Choosing a dog can be difficult. There's research to do, then the work of locating a trustworthy breeder, and perhaps waiting for a puppy to grow old enough to leave his mother and litter-mates behind. If you're adopting from a shelter, you face the sometimes heart-wrenching task of scanning cage after cage full of yearning faces. Rarely does a dog simply walk up to your front door and announce his intention to become your best friend; and even then, you have to decide whether or not to take him up on the offer.

Once you've made your choice, however, your job becomes much more simple. You need to prepare your home for the new arrival. In most cases, only a little time, effort, and expense are required. The best way to prepare your home is to spend a short period each day thinking like a dog. Since this involves a certain suspension of disbelief, some may find the exercise more difficult than others. However, you needn't get down on all fours and root around the cupboards unless you feel it will stimulate your imagination.

A DOG'S-EYE VIEW

Canine physiology and psychology has developed for a single purpose: hunting. Humans share this rather violent instinct, of course. Yet during the course of evolution, the human repertoire broadened to include such impulses as making tools and communicating through speech. Dogs chose a simpler path, and fewer burdens. Nearly all of their mental energy is directed to recognizing prey, tracking it, killing it, and eating it.

When not actively engaged in any of these tasks, dogs spend a good deal of time refining their technique and broadening their knowledge base. Humans tend to call such activity "play," though anyone who has challenged a truly competitive tennis or golf enthusiast can attest to how seriously some individuals take their games. So it is with dogs. Only consistent discipline can convince them to pass up an opportunity to exercise their skills and increase their odds of winning the rough game of survival.

As you prepare your home for a new arrival, two general tendencies relating to the canine hunting instinct bear consideration:

- Anything small enough to be eaten probably will be eaten.
- Any opportunity to explore the world unsupervised will probably be seized.

Failure to recognize either tendency creates a potentially hazardous situation. Your dog may either harm herself, destroy her surroundings, or damage a neighbor's property. Dogs, like children, need boundaries. Without them, they can't tell where they fit in and will likely become nervous or aggressive.

DIVISIONS OF TERRITORY

Ultimately, comfort depends on the establishment of certain routines. As with most species, dogs rely on a sort of internal rhythm to tell them when important events such as feeding, walking, and bedtime are supposed to occur. Due largely to the complexity of modern life, people seem to be more flexible in terms of bargaining with this internal timing mechanism. The relatively uncluttered experience of an average dog, however, admits rather less spontaneity. A schedule laid down at the beginning of their lives in a new home remains fixed in their minds.

In the same way, dogs come to rely on certain territorial regularities. The average person suffers relatively little anxiety over deciding whether to eat at the table, in front of the television, or outdoors under the spreading chestnut tree. Most dogs prefer to eat, sleep, and accomplish other necessary tasks in the same place every day.

Sleeping Areas

Allowing a dog to sleep in your own bed or that of another member of the household is a matter of personal taste. Some authorities advise against the practice. A dog's coat accumulates fleas, ticks, dirt, and other unsavory elements, many of which can pass diseases or otherwise contaminate humans. Ticks, for example, can communicate Lyme disease to both dogs and people. Lice, mites, and other external parasites can cause itching, swelling, and rashes. Still, many people feel that with regular grooming and bathing a dog is no more strange a bedfellow than other creatures.

If you decide Gracie must sleep in her own bed (or if she makes such a determination herself), her sleeping area should be free of drafts and foot traffic, though not altogether cut off from the rest of the household. While dogs generally do not enjoy being left alone for long periods, some can be trained to spend the night in a closed-off room. Compromises of this sort may need to be worked out in the case of an adult dog who has not learned the finer points of household etiquette, or if two dogs fight over territory.

Bear in mind, your dog should not be made to sleep in an area of the home where you would not feel comfortable sleeping. A garage or basement is simply not acceptable, unless the floor and walls have been sealed against dampness and cold. Even so, the garage is particularly unsuitable, since your dog may be exposed to toxic fumes and poisonous substances like antifreeze, paint, and petroleum products.

If you must isolate your dog at night, chances are she will adjust more easily if you place a bowl of water and a bit of food in her sleeping area. A nice rawhide bone can also help to pass the lonely hours. Even so, you may have to put up with a few nights of barking or whining before she fully accepts the notion of being on her own for the night. Since dogs are usually relaxed and sleepy after meals, try offering a bedtime snack. However, if whining continues longer than a week or destructive behavior develops, you may need to reconsider your options.

Gates

It's often wise to confine a young puppy to a certain area of the house when you are not around to supervise her actively. A gate will keep her out of mischief while still allowing her freedom to walk about and to keep an eye on the rest of the house. Gates also serve to confine a dog to a particular room at night while minimizing the sense of rejection or isolation she is bound to suffer. Dog gates should be made of strong wire mesh and tall enough to prevent an ambitious dog of medium size from leaping to freedom. In general, gates designed for children will not suffice.

Doghouses

Hardier breeds that can withstand inclement weather can adapt to life in a doghouse. The house must be constructed solidly enough to protect Rolf from wind, rain, and snow, and you should introduce him to his new quarters as soon as he arrives. Dogs less than a year old should not be left outdoors since their bodies are not developed sufficiently to endure cold or dampness. During the first year, however, they can and should be allowed to spend longer and longer periods in the eventual barracks.

Regardless of age, dogs should not be kept outdoors when they are sick, or during periods of intense cold, rain, or wind. Owners must be prepared to spend a good deal of time outdoors with a dog who lives in a doghouse or pen to remind him of his connection to the family; otherwise, he may begin to see the yard as "his" territory and expect you to defer to his rules whenever you visit.

Eating Areas

Like sleeping quarters, eating areas should be out of the way of regular household traffic. Even the most pleasant dining experience can be ruined by someone walking among the plates. More importantly, dogs often become quite aggressive about their food; many will not hesitate to bite if they feel someone else has designs on their dinner. Young children, especially, must be kept away from dogs at mealtimes, as curiosity may lead to unexpectedly serious consequences. Moreover, you may find that your dog will not suffer other dogs to eat nearby.

Usually, a corner of the kitchen serves handily as an eating area. The refrigerator is nearby and linoleum or tile is handier to clean than carpeting. Because Gracie's table manners may raise eyebrows, you may prefer feeding her in the bathroom or basement, or even outside. She probably won't mind where she eats, so long as the location is consistent.

To Crate or Not to Crate?

The issue of crating has raised some controversy over the past few years. While some people find the idea of confining a dog inside something that looks suspiciously like a prison is cruel and unnecessary, many agree that allowing a dog—especially a very young one—to roam unsupervised through an unfamiliar environment is no less rash than leaving a toddler at home by himself all day. A puppy or a new dog left to its own devices can get into a considerable amount of trouble; some situations may be life-threatening. Like toddlers, dogs are liable to put anything in their mouths in the course of their explorations. By the same token, on their own they are likely to engage in certain activities that would be punished if you were to catch them at it.

Moreover, even the most relentlessly social creature enjoys an opportunity to go off by herself now and again. A crate of one's own provides a welcome refuge from a busy schedule of playing, protecting, investigating, and generally engaging in adorable or outgoing activities. Conveniently located in a corner of the den, kitchen, or living room, a crate affords both privacy and an opportunity to survey the communal area every now and then. A dog who has a crate of her own will also likely spend less time on the furniture, and more readily embrace the idea of not sleeping in her master's bed. She will more readily choose to sleep in her own ''den.''

For the sake of convenience and expense, you'll probably want to purchase a crate large enough to accommodate your puppy when she's fully grown. If the crate is too large, though, a puppy who isn't housebroken may use an extreme corner to relieve herself. A responsible breeder can tell you the right dimensions to suit the breed you've chosen. You can also make the crate more comfortable by lining the bottom with a blanket, rug, or sheet. Whatever padding you choose should be woven tightly enough to withstand attempts at shredding, since swallowed threads or strips of material can cause choking or intestinal problems.

A few other considerations should be taken into account as well. Dogs with long or thick coats tend to suffer in hot or stuffy environments, and therefore feel more comfortable in a well-ventilated crate; short-haired dogs tend to feel the effects of cold more severely and require a crate that offers more protection against drafts. Any wire bars or grating should be strong enough and set closely enough to prevent a strong puppy or a dog with a long muzzle from bending the wires and poking its head through. Many a clever dog has strangled to death as a result. Meanwhile, if you plan to travel with your dog, the crate should conform to regulations stipulated by public transportation carriers.

BEDS, BOWLS, AND BEYOND

While there is nothing inherently suspicious about charging a few more dollars for a cushion covered in handsome fabric, your dog will probably not appreciate the distinction between plaid, paisley, and plain cotton twill. From a canine point of view, function is more important than form. When shopping for things your dog will use every day, bear in mind she will judge her accessories in terms of convenience and comfort. If the satin pillow you've bought for her to sleep on feels too slippery or firm, she won't use it no matter how adorable you tell her she looks. She will appreciate it, however, if you take the time to assemble a few items she can really use.

Collars and Leashes

The type of collar you use will depend on the size and age of your dog. Puppies and small dogs do best with a rolled leather or nylon collar. Older, larger dogs can wear a leather collar around the house or yard; when walking, though, it's a good idea to use a chain-link collar that tightens around the neck when the dog pulls too hard against his leash. Very large dogs (as well as aggressive breeds like German shepherds, Dobermans, and Rottweilers) should wear a metal corrective collar fitted with spurs when taken out in public. The Promise head collar, described in Chapter Six, offers an excellent alternative to a metal corrective collar.

Your dog's collar should be roughly three inches wider than her neck. Anything smaller may choke her, while a collar that is too large may tempt her to slip out. If she succeeds, she might run loose without identification; if she does not, she can choke herself. Certain breeds, such as Pomeranians and chow chows, can't be convinced to wear any sort of collar. In such cases, a harness should be used.

For training purposes, a six-foot leash provides ample control. Leather tends to be gentler on the hands, though nylon or canvas works just as well. A six-foot leash is perfectly suitable for short walks, though for longer adventures you'll probably want a longer leash that retracts and extends with a push of a button.

Dog Beds

Whether you choose to crate or not, it's a good idea to provide a comfortable bed for your dog. The bed may serve to line

Gretchen's crate or to create a cozy resting spot when she prefers to nap in a more public spot. A dedicated dog bed will help keep fur off sofas, armchairs, and other areas of repose, and minimize other sorts of damage as well. Typically, dogs like to pound out a nice hollow before going to sleep. You may observe your own pet turning circles or kneading her chosen spot, behavior that harks back to her wild ancestors, who perforce dug shallow pits in the earth for sleeping. Most importantly, however, a dog tends to rest more peaceably where her own scent has not been contaminated with other markings.

Bowls

As hunters, dogs are particularly conscious of mealtime. Most don't care how prettily their table is laid, so long as it provides easy access to the main attraction. Since dogs typically thrust their faces directly into their food, bowls should be large enough to accommodate the entire snout and sturdy enough to resist tipping. A placemat or sheet of newspaper set beneath the bowl will help contain any bits of food that drop out of your dog's mouth.

Most pet stores sell bowls with flat or rubber-tipped bottoms. Metal or ceramic serves equally well for large- and medium-sized dogs, while smaller breeds can usually manage more delicate settings. Stackable metal bowls can be handy for traveling. Glass, which can easily shatter or chip, should be avoided altogether; accidentally swallowed pieces can cause irreparable damage to your dog's digestive tract.

Whether you provide one bowl for dry food and another for moist rations is up to you. Bowls in which moist food has been served should be washed once daily in order to minimize odors and bacteria. In addition, a separate bowl of fresh water must be available at all times. Dogs are notoriously thirsty animals, and if water is not conveniently provided they will seek satisfaction on their own. Many a hostess has gone red around the collar when her dinner guests are disturbed by the noise of Prince slurping eagerly from the commode.

Toys

Chewing is nature's way of keeping your dog's teeth clean and strong. Puppies, in particular, are apt to gnaw on anything they can find in order to relieve the pain and discomfort of teething; and even as adults they'll continue to do so, if only to exercise their powerful jaw muscles. This behavior is instinctive, inextricably bound up in the hunting impulse, and impossible to suppress. If you don't provide something for your dog to chew on, she'll find a substitute among your possessions.

As with beds and bowls, a bewildering array of dog toys has been made available. Once again, appearance means little to your dog. The best toys, in fact, are simple constructions of rawhide or tough rubber. Though somewhat repulsive to the human eye, they are nonetheless sturdy enough to withstand rough treatment. Avoid small objects or anything comprised of small parts, such as plastic eyes or hands. "Small" is a relative term, of course. A rubber ball around which a Pomeranian can barely wrap its little mouth may be swallowed without a second thought by a Great Dane. Rawhide toys, meanwhile, should be limited to forms that aren't easily shredded; otherwise bits of the toy can be swallowed and become lodged in the intestines.

Even large toys, if made of lightweight materials, can be shredded and swallowed bit by bit. This is especially hazardous in the case of squeaky toys. Dogs derive great pleasure from playing with things that make noise, but the main thrust of their play involves locating the squeaking mechanism and eating it. While all synthetic materials can prove toxic, plastic or metal squeakers are simply not digestible. Removing objects of this sort usually involves surgery.

Finally, avoid offering old socks, shoes, or other personal articles as a substitute for a real toy. Your dog will naturally be drawn by the scent of the rest of your personal effects, and you have no one to blame but yourself if he mistakes your brand-new loafers for a handsome chewie.

Grooming Tools

Though short-haired dogs don't require the same attention to their appearance as longhairs, occasional grooming is warranted, if only for the sake of comfort and cleanliness. At the very least, grooming is an enjoyable and effective means of bonding with your dog. In essence, you assume the role of mother dog, and each grooming session will reinforce your dog's sense of trust in you.

Nail Clippers. Probably the most important tool in any canine beauty kit is a sturdy pair of nail clippers. Human toenail clippers are not suitable, as they tend to simply crush the nail. Canine clippers resemble pliers, with a small slot through which the nail may be inserted; a small blade shoots forth to nip the nail when the handles are squeezed. It's important to accustom your puppy to nail clipping as early as possible, so she will come to accept it as a part of grooming.

Brushes and Combs. Except for very short-haired breeds like French bulldogs, all dogs require a bit of brushing to keep their coats in good order. The type of implement you use will depend on the length of your dog's coat; a breeder or veterinarian can recommend the most appropriate tool for your dog. In general, shorthairs are best groomed with brushes made of short, natural bristles, while rough or long coats typically require a long-toothed wire brush, often called a currycomb.

Unless your dog never goes outside and never comes in contact with other dogs, you'll need to use a very thin-toothed comb—known as a flea comb. Even the most pampered pet is liable to attract fleas and other parasites. These must be rigorously contained, or they will quickly spread not only through your dog's coat, but throughout your home as well. Unless you're particularly nimble, crushing each flea you discover is a tricky occupation; it's far easier to drop the little brutes into a wide-mouthed jar of rubbing alcohol.

While flea powders, sprays, and collars are effective, most do not guarantee complete control. More importantly, such products contain toxic chemicals, so you absolutely must consult your veterinarian before use. However, newer, nontoxic flea control systems are being developed. Ask your veterinarian for information.

Clippers and Strippers. Poodles and other fashionable breeds require clipping now and again to keep their coats in shape. While this is best accomplished by a professional groomer, some owners prefer to do the job themselves. Specially designed electric clippers with rotating heads are available in larger pet stores, or may be purchased at a grooming salon. Terriers and other wire-coat breeds, meanwhile, often need to have their coats trimmed or stripped. Stripping combs, designed with serrated teeth, and similar devices can be obtained from a well-supplied pet store or salon.

Bathing Solutions. It's a rare dog who does not begin to exude a special fragrance after a while. Even dogs less prone to pungency may tramp through mud or snow, or surrender to an impulse to roll in dirt or grass. An occasional bath will remove dirt, germs, and other irritants—as well as minimize the peculiarly "doggy" odor you may no longer notice, but which tends to make occasional visitors acutely uncomfortable. However, because canine skin is more sensitive than human skin, frequent bathing can cause itching, flaking, and other symptoms associated with dryness. Unless Victor has tangled with a skunk or immersed himself in mud, avoid bathing him any more than once a month. Use a mild shampoo specifically formulated for your dog's coat type; it won't sting his eyes or dry his skin. In emergency situations you may resort to baby shampoo, though even formulations of this sort are too harsh for regular use.

Long-haired dogs, especially those with pale or white fur, tend to attract dirt more quickly than short-haired animals. The situation may be remedied by using powder products known as "dry shampoos." These are available at most pet stores and salons, but cornstarch will work just as well. Simply work the powder into the coat and brush it out. A dry bath is also effective for puppies, who should not be bathed until at least six months old.

Unmentionables

If you're adopting a puppy, you will most definitely want to keep a pile of old newspapers handy to cover the floor while he is mastering the subtleties of housebreaking (a subject that will be discussed more completely in the next chapter). Owners of one of the smaller toy breeds may even wish to permanently paper-train their pet. Anyone adopting an adult dog, meanwhile, should probably paper the floors during the first few days after arrival, especially if the dog is coming from a shelter. The proof of housebreaking is in the pudding, so to speak—or more accurately, the lack thereof. Even a normally fastidious adult may become so nervous or disoriented by a change of residence that he forgets his manners.

You'll also need either a scoop or a supply of plastic bags for retrieving solid waste deposited during the daily walk. *There is absolutely no excuse for leaving evidence of your dog's digestion on a sidewalk, street, or lawn.* Piles of waste are not only unsightly; they pose a serious health problem to other dogs, children, and pedestrians with more important things on their minds. Suffice to say that careless owners who do not receive their just reward in this life will be compensated appropriately in the next.

Finally, if you are adopting a female who has either not been spayed or whose reproductive capabilities remain in doubt, you may wish to keep a small supply of canine diapers or feminine protective garments on hand. A well-stocked pet store or veterinarian's office will usually make these available in small, medium, and large sizes. Protective garments will prevent certain discharges associated with her fertile period from staining rugs, furniture, and clothing.

HAZARDS OF OCCUPANCY

As mentioned in the first chapter, most dogs are not strong readers. Their grasp of the spoken word, meanwhile, is typically limited to simple commands, such as Sit, Stay, Heel, and so on. Were you to patiently explain the hazards associated with moving vehicles, for example, most dogs would smile and nod—and dash out into the street as soon as your back was turned. Of course, dogs are capable of learning from their mistakes. However, if the mistake happens to be fatal, it matters little whether they've learned or not.

Examine your home, including the garage and basement, for obvious health hazards such as unprotected windows, toxic chemicals, medications, and heated surfaces. No less treacherous, though less apparent, are small pieces of jewelry, strings, electrical cords, golf balls, and a host of situations associated with the great outdoors. Both types of dangers, as well as related precautions, will be examined below.

Windows

Motion of any kind tends to tweak a dog's territorial instinct. It won't matter to your dog whether the moving object is a squirrel, the neighbor's cat, another dog, or a mail truck. Once his instinct is aroused, he must investigate. The hunting instinct comes into play here as well, particularly if what your dog sees corresponds to one of the major food groups. Watching one toothsome meal after another pass before him, your dog may not be able to contain his desire to break free and claim such fertile territory as his own.

An open window is the devil's doorway. Escape from a ground floor window can have perilous consequences, which will be discussed below. Similar flights from a high-rise apartment window or terrace are almost always fatal. The only way to prevent such tragedy and still enjoy fresh air is to provide secure screens for every window. Screens that snap into the window frame itself, usually interchangeable with storm windows, afford the best protection.

Unfortunately, many apartment buildings don't supply these screens to residents, and even certain homes are fitted with windows that tilt in or out, rather than slide up or down. If you find yourself in this situation, you will have to install a screen or gate. Screens should be made of sturdy, tear-resistant mesh, while gates should be made of metal. Both should be wide and tall enough to encompass the entire window, and securely anchored inside the window frame, rather than between the edge of the window and the sash. A strong or persistent dog will usually find a way to push a loose screen free.

Hot Stuff

Like most animals, dogs seem to comprehend innately the danger of fire. Unfortunately, people rarely cook with fire nowadays unless inspired by some particular eccentricity; and dogs do not innately grasp the danger of a hot stove burner, or an open kettle or frying pan. Curiosity or excitement in the kitchen can cause lasting damage to paws, coat, eyes, and ears. To prevent burns or scalding, teach your dog to avoid leaping on counters and stoves. Do not allow him in the kitchen if you know you'll be carrying hot kettles and roasting pans back and forth; should you stumble or be knocked off balance by an eager helper, you may end up spilling boiling water or hot grease all over your pet.

Similarly, when you've finished pressing your clothes, unplug the iron and leave it cooling in an area inaccessible to your dog. Candles, oil lamps, or alcohol lamps should be extinguished if you intend to leave the room for more than a moment; through clumsiness or curiosity, your dog may singe his face or fur, or even start a fire. Especially avoid setting flammable items on any table at tail-wagging level, which is apt to be swept clean on a regular basis. (Toxic and breakable items should also be placed out of tail's reach.)

Smokers should never leave a lit cigarette burning in the ashtray while running to answer the phone or handle an emergency. Even after extinguishing your cigarette, it's still a good idea to empty the ashtray immediately, or remove it from the purview of a curious pet.

Household Toxins

Though laundry detergent and other cleaning agents don't seem especially enticing to an adult person, dogs—like children—are inclined to taste everything they can. Cartoon fantasies depict the consequences of swallowing soaps and other cleaning products as a tendency to hiccup bubbles. The real-life outcome is far less amusing. Detergents can sear the lining of your dog's esophagus and release harsh chemicals into his system, causing severe vomiting, stomach bleeding, blindness, and organ failure. Tragedies of this kind can be prevented by simply attaching a childproof latch to any cupboard or cabinet that contains harmful substances. In addition, never leave open containers of cleaning fluid or powder unattended on the floor or counter.

By the same token, prescription drugs and over-the-counter remedies should be stored out of reach, preferably in a securely latched cabinet. Even cough drops and vitamins, if ingested in quantity, can poison your pet. Insecticides, flypaper, roach traps, rodent bait, and similar products should likewise be set out only in areas where your dog cannot possibly come into contact with them. Since most bait gives off a sweet smell to attract vermin, your dog is likely to devise any number of cunning strategies to retrieve traps of this kind.

Less obvious threats include ballpoint pen ink, matches, shampoo, cosmetics, skin care products, deodorants, and perfumes. Paint, paint thinners, putty, plaster, and similar products can also pose a threat to your dog's health. In the course of traipsing through a home-improvement project or investigating a cupboard, Rollo may accidentally come into contact with one or another of these substances, which can irritate his skin. Worse, when he licks himself, he will ingest these poisons.

Chocolate

Theobromine, a chemical compound found in chocolate, is extremely toxic to dogs. It can trigger epileptic seizures, or cause cardiac arrhythmia and possible heart attack. It may irritate your dog's digestive tract, causing internal bleeding. The chances of survival depend on a combination of factors, including the dog's size and weight, and any preexisting medical conditions. Even if only a small amount of chocolate has been eaten, take the dog to a veterinarian or clinic immediately.

Plants

Dogs sometimes eat grass or plant leaves. Various explanations have been offered, ranging from simple curiosity to a yearning for roughage. Puppies, of course, will chew on anything. Unfortunately, many indoor and outdoor plants have a deleterious effect on dogs. Common hazards include philodendron, poinsettia, iris, morning glory, tomato, and lily of the valley. A more complete list can be found in Appendix C. Indoor plants should be hung high or placed on inaccessible shelves.

Outdoor gardens pose a more ticklish problem, since dogs like to dig in flower and vegetable beds, and to mark bushes, shrubbery, and other flora with urine. Erecting a fence around flower and vegetable gardens, while ideal from a protective point of view, is not necessarily an aesthetically pleasing solution. Owners should therefore supervise early visits to the back or front yard, and immediately reprimand dogs who approach the flower beds and vegetable gardens.

Cords and Strings

String, yarn, ribbons, and thread are fun to chew on. Unfortunately, your dog can choke on them, and if ingested in sufficient quantity, strings of any sort can cause intestinal blockage. Electrical cords are especially dangerous. While puppies are teething, it's best to unplug electrical cords and either tie them or wrap them around the base of the appliance to which they're connected whenever you're not around to supervise. Even after a puppy is grown, the temptation to chew electric cords may remain. Reprimand all instances immediately (see Chapter Six for the most appropriate methods of discouraging behavior) and remove him from the vicinity. If the problem persists, wrap the cords in electrical tape or enclose them in plastic or rubber tubing, available at many hardware stores.

Sharp Things and Foreign Objects

Keep pins, needles, tacks, staples, and other sharp objects in suitable containers, or discard them after use. Dogs can easily damage their paws by treading on something sharp, or tear their mouths and throats by chewing on them. Earrings, broaches, and other bits of jewelry should also be stored out of harm's way. Knives and scissors should be returned to their proper homes after use, as a sharp blade can cause considerable damage to an eye or a paw. Fragments of broken glass or porcelain should be swept or vacuumed immediately, and the floor should be wiped with a damp rag or paper towel.

Assorted objects such as golf balls, rubber bands, baby bottle nipples, marbles, and diminutive decorative items should never be left where dogs can retrieve them. Similarly, dogs should be either restricted from or closely watched in areas where children are playing with small toys, such as Lego, or games that involve small pieces. Pens, pencils, erasers, and other writing paraphernalia belong in their proper places.

The scent of food scraps, meanwhile, exerts a powerful influence. Dogs are not shy about investigating garbage, so receptacles should be tightly covered or stored in a latched cupboard. In particular, bones of all varieties should be kept well out of reach, since they can splinter and lodge in a dog's throat or stomach. Other objects, such as Q-Tips, cardboard tubes, tissues, and razor blades can prove equally disastrous.

Stairs

Most dogs can negotiate a sensible staircase fairly easily. Circular staircases may present problems for both large and small dogs; the former may find it hard to manage a hairpin turn at even moderate speed, while the latter might easily slide through ladderlike steps. Old dogs, puppies, and toys, meanwhile, should avoid stairs of any sort. While the ascent may not pose particular problems, the descent can be tricky for those with short legs or arthritic joints. It is best to keep a gate at the bottom of the stairs to prevent any furtive assaults on the upper stories, and one at the top of the stairs if Jasper is allowed to snooze at your feet at night.

THE GREAT OUTDOORS

Almost any dog will go mad without fresh air and exercise. Unlike most other household pets, dogs do not pass quietly beyond the confines of sanity. A dog on the verge of emotional collapse will shred, tear, chew, bark, whine, howl, urinate, defecate, and make frantic efforts to escape the prison his home has become. Long before such behavior reaches its peak, the sensible owner will take Wolfgang for a walk. Unfortunately, a host of dangers awaits him in the outside world. These include:

- Automobiles
- Bicycles
- Other dogs

- Wild animals
- Toxic chemicals
- Ticks and other parasites
- The dreaded dogcatcher

The Blessing of Restraint

For their own protection and your own peace of mind, dogs should always be walked on a leash—even if they've been trained to behave off-leash. The only exception to this rule applies when you take your dog to a dog run in a local park or public area.

Of course, many owners like to set their dogs free during a trip to the beach or an outing in the country. In areas where leash laws do not apply, this is a matter of personal conscience. More than one dog has drowned at the seaside, or disturbed other sunbathers, while gulping down a few buckets' worth of polluted salt water can cause dehydration or toxic reactions. And even confident owners may be startled by the speed with which their dogs give chase to a squirrel, another dog, or a shiny red convertible.

Probably the most serious hazard an unleashed dog faces is a moving automobile. With the exception of Seeing Eye dogs, most animals cannot be taught to look both ways before crossing the street. Particularly when presented with an opportunity to harrow the neighbor's cat or some other small creature, no dog worth the name is going to keep an eye out for oncoming traffic. Moving vehicles are the primary cause of death among dogs.

The sight of a moving bicycle, meanwhile, tends to provoke most dogs beyond all rhyme or reason. A mad dash after a bicycle can lead directly into the path of an oncoming truck. At the very least, a furious chase can terrify whoever happens to be riding the bike; if an accident occurs as a result, you will be responsible not only for medical and property damages, but perhaps even for a human life. Finally, in his attempt to overpower the bicycle, your dog may become tangled in the wheels or chains and bring serious injury upon himself.

Wandering

Dogs love to roam. Should your dog give into wanderlust while off-leash, he may face hazards in addition to traffic. Other dogs, for example, may mistake his appearance for an invasion of territory and challenge him to a fight. Wild animals do not take kindly to either simple curiosity or outright attack, and if your dog comes up against a more powerful creature, he may be seriously wounded, killed, or infected with rabies. Rabies is fatal to both animals and people; the early stages of the disease are difficult to discern, and your dog may not show symptoms until he poses a serious threat to you, your family, or neighbors. Rabid dogs must be destroyed.

Toxic substances present another health hazard, whether disposed of improperly, or casually piled in neighboring yards. Rat poison, for example, is often laid in public parks. Antifreeze in your own or a neighbor's driveway is especially dangerous, because it smells and tastes rather sweet. If swallowed, even a small amount can be deadly.

Fleas, ticks, and mosquitoes are common problems in both rural and suburban settings. Aside from being notoriously difficult to control, fleas are also host to tapeworms. Ticks can latch onto your dog, possibly infecting him with Lyme disease and other diseases; and ticks can easily transfer themselves from dogs to owners. Mosquitoes can transmit heartworm, one of the most deadly of all canine parasites.

A wandering dog can also damage your neighbor's property, as well as injure or frighten pedestrians. If your homeowner's policy does not cover liability for damage caused by your pet, you should invest in liability insurance. Acts of canine vandalism or hooliganism, meanwhile, generate an air of tension throughout the neighborhood. While you are both morally and financially responsible for any damage done by your dog, your neighbors cannot be held legally accountable for laying out poison, or shooting a dog who invades their chicken coop or chases their cattle.

Fences

Fences serve not only to keep your dog in the yard, but to prevent other dogs and uninvited persons from accosting your dog. Unfortunately, the most common type of fence available stands only three- or four-feet high—inadequate both in terms of restraint or protection. While toys, puppies, and small breeds may be prevented from leaping over the top of a four-foot fence, most other dogs will only laugh.

Before investing in a more impressive barrier, you may wish to consider stringing aluminum cans along both sides of the fence. The noise resulting from any attempt to climb the fence is usually quite discouraging; if you're home, the sound will alert you to an attempted flight or invasion. You might also try stringing heavy gauge wire along the fence to inhibit climbing, or lining the fence with corrugated fiberglass. Some dogs—terriers in particular—are adept at digging underneath fences. Attempted flights of this nature may be foiled by laying concrete, paving stones, or gravel along the border of the fence.

Sadly, none of these solutions will deter a large or determined medium-sized dog from simply taking a running leap over the fence. In such cases, you will either have to erect a taller fence, or install an "invisible" or electric fence to fortify an existing structure.

Electric Fences. An electrified wire strung across the top of a fence will usually provide enough of a shock to discourage dogs adept at climbing fences. Electric wires must be run through insulators, unless they are attached to completely nonconductive supports. Fiberglass is probably the most reliable nonconductive material; even wood may become conductive if wet. Puppies should not be exposed to electrified fences, as the shock may kill them, burn them, or cause serious internal damage.

Digging may be discouraged by burying an electric wire along the fence border. However, not all wire is suitable for burying. The wrong type of wire can short or cause a fire. Before electrifying an existing fence, consult a professional. Better yet, hire one.

Invisible Fences. Costly but effective, invisible fences involve underground wires and radio-receptive collars. If your dog wanders too close to the wire, the collar emits a high-pitched warning signal; should Bobo ignore the initial warning and venture closer to the forbidden zone, the collar will deliver a shock. Owners who prefer an unobstructed view of the yard will likely appreciate the advantage of a fence of this sort. Invisible fences also serve to discourage dogs in a fenced yard from approaching flower and vegetable beds.

Certain disadvantages may not be apparent at first glance, however. For example, two or three weeks of specialized training is usually required before your dog will understand the significance of the warning signal and any subsequent shock he receives. More importantly, though an invisible fence may prevent your dog from wandering, it will not deter thieves, strange dogs, and other unsavory types from entering your yard. Finally, should your dog somehow elude the invisible barrier, she won't be able to return to the yard once her desire to roam has faded; her collar will deliver a shock no matter which side of the fence she finds herself on.

SUMMARY

If you're reading this book, chances are you already have a strong sense of duty and an abiding love for animals. The material in this chapter is intended not to frighten you, but simply to alert you to situations you might not ordinarily recognize. Objects and events that pose a danger to your dog may not necessarily coincide with hazards to your own health.

From the moment you bring your dog home, you are entirely accountable for her well-being. Once you've taken reasonable precautions, however, you probably won't have to repeat the process. As dogs mature, their temperaments tend to mellow; curiosity fades somewhat, and the eagerness to taste or chew whatever happens across their path diminishes accordingly. At the end of a year, most owners can relax, reconnect their lamps and other electric appliances, and go back to leaving their shoes and socks in the hall.

Chapter 5

The Blessed Event

After all the time and effort you've invested in research, selection, and preparation, the best thing you can do before bringing your new companion home is to spend a few days quietly relaxing. Dogs are extremely sensitive to the tone of their surroundings. This is not a paranormal ability. Dogs simply pay attention to sensory details that most people take for granted. They "read" sounds, scents, and gestures the way people read newspapers. Naturally, certain individuals will resent learning that their inner lives are completely obvious to a dog. Most others find the lesson quite useful.

By this time you've probably built up certain expectations about the new arrival. If you attach too much value to them, you're bound to be disappointed in some fashion. Like all living creatures, dogs rarely behave in the flesh as perfectly as they do in daydreams. More significantly, they rarely spend their idle moments thinking about being adopted. So, while you've generated a lot of anticipation over the adoption, chances are your new dog won't have the faintest idea of the momentous change about to take place in his life.

As a result, he may experience some anxiety or discomfort during the first few days or weeks in his new surroundings; he almost certainly won't behave the way you imagined he would. You'll only make matters worse by judging his actual behavior against your expectations. Although it will be necessary to lay out a few basic ground rules and stand by them, you can also take certain steps to make this time of transition as encouraging as possible.

THE JOURNEY HOME

Unless your home is a short distance from your new dog's previous residence, you will almost certainly need to transport her by car or some form of public conveyance. This is especially important if you're bringing home a puppy who has not received her full round of vaccinations—usually between the ages of twelve and fifteen weeks. Until she is vaccinated, she remains vulnerable to certain viruses and other unwholesome organisms, and must not be allowed outside.

At the same time, puppies who have never traveled won't necessarily understand the speed and noise associated with a car or other vehicle. Even older dogs may not have traveled extensively—or if they have, their previous experiences may have been less than satisfying. At the very least, driving away from home and hearth with a comparative stranger can be a traumatic or confusing experience.

For your dog's safety as well as your own, it is essential during this first trip together to confine her to a carrier or crate. She will feel much more secure riding in her own coach, so to speak, than slipping and sliding all over the backseat. If she's free to roam about the car, she may try to jump in your lap or hide at your feet—either of which may impair your driving. With time, of course, you'll be able to travel together more intimately. At present, you don't know her well enough to predict what will provoke anxiety and what will not, so it's wiser to err on the side of caution.

If you're adopting from a home, find out in advance if the breeder or previous owner can provide you with a crate or carrier your dog has used in the past. Canine senses become especially keen in moments of stress, and Mitzi will feel more comfortable in something familiar. If a carrier is not available, or if you're adopting from a store or a shelter, try to bring along a toy she likes or a piece of her old bedding.

You will also need to line the bottom of the carrier with newspaper or a towel, in case your dog soils herself or becomes nauseous. Some dogs, like some people, get carsick. You can help to avoid such unpleasantness by not feeding her five hours prior to travel.

If you're driving home with your new companion, consider taking someone along to talk to her during the trip home, and to hold the carrier if you're transporting a puppy or a small dog. Dogs take great comfort in soothing speech, and the warmth and smell of a human body. Car windows are best kept closed to minimize traffic noises. In fact, even after your dog has become accustomed to traveling without a carrier, car windows should never be opened wide enough for your dog to poke her head out. She may very well suffer injury from a passing vehicle, or snap at a presumptuous admirer.

It is somewhat less common to transport a large dog on a public bus or train. Before doing so, consult the transit authority in your area for specific guidelines; or consider asking a friend to drive you. Transporting a small dog or puppy tends to be a simpler operation, since you can hold the carrier on your lap. You will need to keep up a steady stream of soothing conversation with your dog, since the number of scents and sounds confronting her during the ride home may very likely overwhelm her. Avoid pushing your fingers inside the carrier or placing your face too close to the grate. When anxious, your dog may respond in an aggressive manner you will both regret.

Walking home with your new friend is the least agreeable option. Obedience is as much a matter of trust as training, and you simply don't know each other well enough at this point to rely on your ability to command. If you absolutely must walk, use a short leash and a choke chain collar, the better to restrain her should another dog appear on the scene, or her eagerness to investigate her surroundings prove too strong.

HOME AT LAST

Allow plenty of time for your dog to adjust to his new surroundings. In addition to any loneliness or anxiety he may feel, his senses will be working overtime. A bewildering array of unfamiliar scents, sights, and sounds must be investigated, identified, and catalogued in his memory. Bear in mind that the canine sensory apparatus is far more subtle and delicate than the human. Whereas people tend to absorb new situations in rather general sweeps, dogs are naturally inclined to examine things more specifically—constructing a holographic sensory image, detail by detail.

Your dog's body language will, in most cases, communicate his responses quite specifically. In particular, pay attention to his tail and ears. These areas of a dog's body express a number of moods and attitudes, as indicated below.

A Few Common Canine Expressions

Tail:

Held horizontally or relaxed.

I'm fine, thank you.

Raised.

Something great is about to happen, I can just feel it! Also, alarm or attention.

Lowered between the legs.

I don't like this situation very much. Alternatively: I'm so ashamed. (Submissive behavior.)

Wagging.

Hi there, how are you? Happy to see you.

Ears:

Raised or, in the case of flop-ears, hanging loosely.

I'm listening, I'm confident, alert.

Pointed in a certain direction, or in the case of flop-ears, raised as high as possible.

What's that? Something interesting going on over there.

Flattened sideways or back.

I'd keep my distance if I were you. (Fear, defensiveness.)

Face:

Lips relaxed, mouth open.	*I like you. I like being alive. I like the way your shoes smell. I can't think of anything I don't like at the moment.*
Lips relaxed, mouth closed.	*Just meditating, don't mind me.*
Lips drawn back tightly.	*I don't know you, and I don't think I want to.*
Lips drawn back, teeth exposed.	*I warned you and you didn't listen. Now you're going to pay. (This represents an exceedingly dangerous situation.)*

Other Signals:

Hair raised along the nape and/or the back.	*Danger. Danger. Danger.*
Growling.	*Don't come one step closer.*
Licking.	*I love you, I adore you. Alternatively: I like the way you smell, now how do you taste?*
Jumping around excitedly.	*Hi, hi, hi!*

Any of these signals can be used in combination to enhance or modify a given message. For example, jumping up and down and licking effectively demonstrates great pleasure at the arrival of a beloved friend, while jumping, growling, and baring teeth sends a rather unequivocal warning against approach.

One Room at a Time

When you arrive home, place your dog's carrier in the room or area you have chosen as his primary quarters—usually the place where he will sleep. Depending on his mood or anxiety level, you may or may not want to introduce other members of the household at this time. If other members of the household are present, advise them to speak gently and not make any sudden movements. By no means should they accost the new arrival. Rather, they should simply hold a hand out and allow the dog to sniff it.

Once he's finished investigating his primary quarters, you can allow him to explore the rest of your home. (Of course, if your home consists of a single room, there won't be much else to explore except the bathroom and possibly the kitchenette.) If possible, let him explore each room thoroughly before moving on to the next. This may not be possible in all residences, in which case you may let him wander at his own pace.

Since an essential part of your dog's initial exploration consists of appreciating certain boundaries, you will need to accompany him around the home, indicating where he may sit, lie, and so forth, and where he may not. Training will be covered in more detail in Chapter Six. Suffice it to say, at this point, that individuals prone to hysterics, agitation, or extreme attachment to material goods should not participate in this crucial early stage of adjustment. Be firm but gentle in your instruction, especially if you're dealing with a puppy. Puppies are merely babies, after all, and psychically quite vulnerable to harshness or reproach. Nevertheless, they bear closer monitoring than older dogs, as their toilet etiquette may not have been firmly established.

Children may need instruction in the appropriate method of lifting and holding a small dog or puppy. In fact, it's a good idea to have them watch a video on puppy training before actually being introduced to a new companion. When handling puppies, great tenderness should be observed at all times. Any attempt to lift him by the scruff of the neck, for example, will inflict great pain; hoisting him by his front paws may cause injury. The accepted method is to slide one hand around the chest, under his front paws, while supporting his back feet with the other hand.

His back should rest comfortably in the crook of the arm that holds the back paws. Many puppies and small dogs enjoy being cradled like an infant. Larger dogs may find the position rather awkward and unpleasant.

Younger children, especially, need to be warned against hanging on too tightly if the dog doesn't want to be held. It should be made clear to them that dogs have sharp teeth and powerful jaws, and will use them to escape a stranglehold. Children must also understand that dogs do not as a rule enjoy being dragged around by their front paws or tails, and rarely sit still at tea parties. Fetching, tugging a hank of rope, chasing, or running are the preferred methods of interaction.

If You're Adopting a Puppy

It takes a lot of work to raise a puppy. During housebreaking, they must be walked several times a day. Training is mandatory, and requires not only the fortitude to withstand hours of repeating commands, but also the patience to handle a rather limited attention span. In addition, you will have to deal with a variety of unruly puppy behaviors, such as teething, begging, rifling the garbage, and jumping up on inappropriate surfaces.

Puppies bond very tightly with their mothers and litter-mates, and will almost certainly feel sad and frightened to find themselves alone for the first time in their lives. More than likely, no one in his new home looks or smells even remotely like a dog. Do your best to soothe a little one by talking to him, stroking him, and holding him when he cries. He needs a great deal of warm and gentle interaction; praise him often, and let him crawl onto your lap when he's tired or frightened. If he hangs cowering in a corner, though, let him be. Pet him only when he ventures forth, or else you'll reinforce timid behavior.

On the other hand, your puppy may feel confident enough to leap into the fray and participate in all household activities. Be careful not to overstimulate him; passing out too many toys or introducing him to too many people at once can wipe him out for a couple of days. Give him ample quiet time to rest and observe. Likewise, since puppies need a great deal of sleep, don't force him to play or wake him up to meet every adoring magi*or neighbor who drops by.

Your puppy will need three or four meals a day, followed by water. Don't be offended if he doesn't touch or finish all his food;

he may be too nervous to eat. Give him twenty or thirty minutes' time alone, and if he doesn't finish, clean out his dish and give him some water anyway. Depending on whether he's old enough to go outside, you'll need to lay out papers or take him for a short walk. Housebreaking, feeding, and walking schedules will be discussed more fully later on in this chapter.

Nighttime can be hard on a puppy. Everyone will sleep better if you keep his crate, carrier, or bed in the same room where you sleep. If this is not possible, or undesirable, confine him to a small area such as the kitchen or bathroom. You might want to consider wrapping a warm water bottle in a towel and placing it conveniently in his bedding. A clock with a satisfying tick may be similarly employed.

Bear in mind that he will probably have to relieve himself two or three times in the middle of the night, and will likely whine or bark to alert you to this need. If he's paper-trained, take him to his spot and return him to his crate or enclosure when he's finished. If he's housebroken, you'll have to find his leash and take him outside for a quick turn around the front yard.

A puppy needs a good deal of attention, so plan on devoting most of his waking hours to wrestling, chasing, and tossing rubber balls. Frequent play periods will build a lasting bond of trust and love, and probably tire your puppy out long enough so that you can get some work done around the house. All too soon, he'll outgrow this sweet, unconditional longing for your company, so cherish the opportunity to indulge him while you may.

If You're Adopting an Older Dog

First of all, you deserve abundant praise for your compassion. Many people prefer adopting puppies, responding either to their indisputable appeal or to the assumption that young dogs are easier to mold. Yet, although puppies are usually more impressionable—and thus more open to correction—than older dogs, no one can predict individual temperament. An adorable puppy is equally likely to mature into a stubborn adult as an obedient one. There is a great deal to be said for choosing a companion whose disposition has been tested by time.

Older dogs offer their new owners other substantial benefits. Because training and experience have fitted them to adjust to new situations, they require less supervision and reassurance than puppies. In addition, most older dogs are housebroken, so you won't have to get up every few hours at night to attend to certain physical needs. If your dog has received some training, your situation becomes even easier, because he will understand at least rudimentary commands. At night, you may only have to show him his bed; if he tries to follow you into yours, a simple "No" or "Stay" should resolve the issue rather quickly. He may whine a bit over spending the night removed from other members of his new family, but his loneliness should diminish once he's sure you'll still be around come morning.

Still, even older dogs may show signs of anxiety or confusion when thrust into a strange environment. Those who felt particular devotion toward their former owners may become depressed, lethargic, or nervous. Those who have suffered abuse or neglect may fear contact of any sort, and may run from loud noises or heavy household traffic. Some dogs have suffered so severely at the hands of their previous owners that they may never fully regain their capacity for trust.

If an older dog exhibits these or similar symptoms, don't try to force your presence or any other demands on him. An atmosphere of security and calmness will, in most cases, draw him out. Use a gentle and encouraging tone when you address him, and, at least while you are at home, allow him to come to you when he feels ready. Though he may never display the same confidence or exuberance you see in other dogs, the bond between you will probably be all the more profound because it is based on acceptance of his frailties. Simply, the love of a shy or suffering animal has no equal in this world.

Other Dogs in the Household

You may find it helpful to postpone introducing the new arrival to other canine residents until after he has explored his territory for a while, and met the human members of the household. In this way, he will gain a certain amount of confidence in his surroundings, as well as a basic appreciation of his standing in relation to you and the other people in the house. During the first few days after the introduction, avoid leaving an established dog alone with a newcomer; your presence may be the only grounds for peaceful coexistence. If your schedule does not allow your continued presence in the house, confine the dogs to separate areas before you leave. You can also minimize or avoid unpleasant confrontations by providing each dog with his own food and water bowls, and by showing no partiality to either the newcomer or the established dog.

If you're bringing a puppy or a young dog into a home already occupied by an older dog, the period of adjustment is usually short and free of conflict: The puppy's place in the hierarchy of the pack is abundantly clear to all concerned. As the youngest and weakest member of the clan, he will almost certainly defer to the strength and wisdom of the older dog. Bear in mind, however, that certain toy breeds have no concept of their size, and may attempt to assert themselves in a manner most unbecoming. Adult terriers, meanwhile, do not always look kindly upon dogs of any age or size who dare to cross their path. It is therefore important to monitor early encounters quite closely.

While a dog's ability to assess rank is usually quite subtle and immediate, you may run into difficulties introducing a dog of about the same age or older than the one who has enjoyed sole tenancy. Females, too, occasionally take offense at the intrusion of a younger female or female puppy. Until the pecking order has been sorted out, you can expect some growling, snapping, and fighting. Ideally, rank will be determined after one or two encounters, at the end of which one or the other dog will surrender. Life rarely conforms to the ideal, however, and you may have to put up with weeks or months of bad temper.

On no account should you attempt to physically separate fighting dogs near the face, head, or neck, unless you relish the idea of a nasty bite. Whenever possible, enlist the aid of another person, each grabbing the back foot or feet of the combatants and upsetting their balance. Note, however, that this method is not often effective in cases of a fight between two large dogs. Alternative techniques involve startling the combatants with a spray of cold water or a loud, unpleasant noise. Another possibility is to call out a command to which you know your dog will respond without question, granting him an opportunity to retreat with dignity.

Dogs and Other Animals

When introducing your new dog to an animal of another species, remember her wild nature. The canine hunting instinct may be compared with the bass line of a song or symphony, which remains steady even when not readily distinguishable, no matter what melodies and harmonies play above it. Likewise, a dog's hunting instinct is the foundation upon which individual character, in all its delightful variety, unfolds.

In general, animals that correspond to a dog's natural prey will not be immediately accepted as companions. Mice, gerbils, guinea pigs, and even rabbits should be kept secured, and allowed to wander loose only when your dog is occupied elsewhere. Parakeets and other birds accustomed to flying around the house on occasion may similarly waken Gracie's wild instinct from domestic slumber. Undoubtedly, a dog can learn to tolerate and even care for animals which, under ordinary circumstances, would be viewed as a toothsome snack. Friendships of this kind must be allowed to develop only under intense scrutiny, however, and are most successfully facilitated by persons blessed with an instinctive feel for animal prejudices and sympathies.

Relations between dogs and cats deserve special consideration, since it is unarguably cruel to confine one or the other to a cage during the entire period of shared residence. Cartoon fantasies aside, dogs and cats do not detest one another on sight. Unpleasantness usually stems from a misinterpretation of common body signals. Whereas a dog wags its tail to suggest friendliness, for example, cats do so when they're confused or irritated. Likewise, cats typically understand quick movements as aggressive behavior, while dogs see leaping or jumping as an invitation to play.

Kittens and puppies raised together often come to understand each other fairly quickly, while their natural exuberance smooths over occasional differences of opinion. Older dogs rarely perceive resident kittens as any threat to their authority, so long as the little ones do not insist on pulling rank. Older cats, meanwhile, can develop at least some tolerance toward puppies introduced into the home, although a young dog's playfulness and curiosity may be construed as impertinence. However, adult felines will usually object strongly to the presence of an older dog. As each absorbs traces of the other's scent, a relationship of strained courtesy will usually develop over time. While it is by no means impossible for a deeper friendship to grow from such unlikely roots, you may have to resign yourself to maintaining a reluctant and fragile truce.

As with other animals, early encounters between cats and dogs of any age must be closely monitored. In particular, watch your cat for hissing and growling, which often precede an attack. A quick slash with a razor-sharp claw can do untold damage to your dog's eye or other parts of his face. Ask your veterinarian or a breeder whether the breeds in question have a history of mutual tolerance or intolerance. Terriers, for example, seem to have great difficulty containing their aggressive instincts, whether confronting cats, rats, or other dogs. Surprisingly, very large breeds tend to display greater tolerance toward smaller creatures—although, if provoked, they probably won't suffer regret over swallowing a bunny or snapping the neck of an arrogant puss.

THE FIRST MONTH

Puppies aren't really ready for adoption until they're seven or eight weeks old. By this age, they have begun to master the subtleties of muscular coordination and are capable of expressing themselves vocally and physically. Through daily contact with litter-mates, parents, and caretakers, they have learned the rudiments of affectionate and aggressive behavior. Now the real work of socialization begins, as they discover the difference between playtime and serious activities. During this stage, puppies begin to understand their strength and learn its limits. Curiosity drives them to test the boundaries of their world. Their eagerness to learn makes them outgoing and extremely responsive to authority.

Popular misconception to the contrary, it is entirely possible to teach an old dog new tricks—if he's been well trained prior to adoption. Unfortunately, the results of inconsistent, ineffective, or just plain bad training can be difficult to reverse. An ill-trained dog may prove resistant to command, or simply unable to adapt to a new and more consistent etiquette. Meanwhile, puppies who have not enjoyed much human contact during the first seven or eight weeks of life are apt to remain somewhat shy around people. In such cases, you'll need to consult a professional trainer or ask your veterinarian to suggest appropriate means of discipline or instruction.

Older dogs who have been abused or suffer some psychological disturbance may become so aggressive as to pose a threat to you, your family, and your neighbors. In rare cases, the only option may be euthanasia administered by a veterinarian. Should a dog prove entirely unmanageable, request assistance from your local ASPCA or pound; they may know someone experienced enough to care for such a dog. Never take it upon yourself to destroy a dog, unless a life stands in immediate jeopardy.

Overcoming the effects of bad training or inadequate socialization requires patience and persistence. Bear in mind that when

Fluffy does something unacceptable, she is not a bad dog: She's a good dog who has suffered neglect or abuse on a scale you can't conceive. Even more than a properly trained dog, she needs your love and acceptance.

Licensing

As mentioned in Chapter One, if you adopt your dog from a pound or shelter, you won't be able to leave without a license for him. If you're adopting an older dog from a home, chances are he will already be licensed. If he's not, or if you're adopting a puppy, you will need to contact your local humane society at once for information on fees, terms, and conditions. Do not wait any longer than the day after bringing your dog home to take care of this important task.

First Visit to the Vet

Ideally, you should have your new dog or puppy examined by a veterinarian within a week of adoption. Even if the previous owner has surrendered all pertinent medical records, nothing can substitute for direct assessment of your dog's health. You will also benefit from establishing a rapport with the veterinarian. If you have your dog's medical records, bring them along so the veterinarian can decide whether or not vaccinations or boosters are necessary. Further information on vaccinations can be found in Chapter Six.

Friends or neighbors may be able to recommend a veterinarian with whom they feel comfortable. In making your choice, consider the following factors:

- Accreditation by a state or national veterinary association
- Convenient location
- Reasonable office hours
- Sanitary conditions of the office or clinic
- Twenty-four-hour emergency service coverage

Don't be shy about asking questions. It's important to establish a good rapport with your veterinarian, since your dog's health will rest in his hands for many years to come.

During the initial visit, the veterinarian will check your dog's body temperature, teeth, and eyes, as well as examine his coat for fleas and his ears for mites. At this point, you can also address any health concerns you may have regarding your dog—for example, if he seems listless or nervous. You should also ask about diseases common to your dog's breed. Golden retrievers, for instance, are prone to a malformation of the hip joint known as hip dysplasia, while many varieties of spaniel are prone to deterioration of the retina. In the course of your research, you will no doubt discover this type of information. However, your veterinarian will be able to discuss breed-specific illnesses in greater detail.

When you make the appointment, let the receptionist know that this is your dog's first visit, and ask whether a stool sample will be necessary. A sample is often required to determine the presence of worms and other internal parasites. Quite often, puppies are born with a roundworm infestation if the mother is similarly infected. A reliable breeder will deworm puppies at regular intervals between the ages of two and six weeks. They should undergo treatment again between the ages of twelve and sixteen weeks, and once more at eight months. Tapeworm infestation is only slightly less common, and must be treated promptly. Worms and other parasites will be discussed more fully in Chapter Six.

As traveling together is still a novel experience, you will probably need to use a carrier or crate. You can leave it behind in the car, provided your dog has already received a full round of vaccinations and you are reasonably sure of your ability to control him on a short leash. Don't take unnecessary risks, however. A sick dog in the waiting room may easily infect your own. Once seated in the waiting room, keep your dog at your side or in your lap at all times.

Many dogs forgive the prodding and poking associated with a routine examination. Others view thermometers and needles with justifiable suspicion. Regardless of the way your dog responds, give him a treat when you return home. Avoid the temptation to offer a reward as you get into the car; it may be promptly regurgitated—an event that rarely inspires feelings of delight in either dogs or owners.

Housebreaking

Housebreaking builds on a dog's innate fastidiousness. Mother dogs keep their pups scrupulously clean, licking them to stimulate elimination and promptly wiping away such small quantities of waste matter as inevitably manifests. Between two and three weeks old, puppies make it a point to relieve themselves away from sleeping and feeding areas. By the time they've completed their vaccinations, they're ready—and usually quite willing—to learn one of the prime advantages of the world beyond the front door.

In the beginning, you will have to keep an eye out for signs of imminent elimination. These often entail a fair amount of whining, pawing the ground, turning in circles, or restless wandering. Try to catch him before he actually squats, or you may end up with an unpleasant stain on your person. The first few times, you may have to physically carry him to the door. If you accompany this activity with a short command, such as "Out" or "Outside," he will make the association quickly enough, and he will follow you to the door when you give the command.

Consistency is essential in the early stages of housebreaking. Use the same door and the same path to the door every time you go out, and bring your puppy to the same spot to relieve himself. Doing so will help minimize confusion or distractions along the way, fixing the main event more firmly in your puppy's mind. Many people use simple verbal commands with this process. For example, they associate the command "Outside" with going to the door, and a short phrase like "Do it" or "Hurry up" with the actual business of relief. Maintaining a reliable feeding and walking schedule, as discussed below, will also serve to make elimination a more predictable occurrence.

Housebreaking requires patience and vigilance. When you're not available or fail to notice your puppy's needs, you can't fault him for making the best of a difficult situation. Any attempt at correction or punishment after the fact is pointless, and will only frighten him. After two or three weeks of consistent effort, you will likely have no cause for alarm or complaint.

Always check with the veterinarian before taking a puppy outside for the first time. In general, this should occur between eight and twelve weeks, although many veterinarians advise against outdoor activities until a puppy has received her final round of vaccinations, usually between the ages of twelve and sixteen weeks. Although more common in urban settings, this rule sometimes applies in rural areas as well. Always follow the guidelines set down by your veterinarian.

If you're adopting an older dog, chances are someone else will have gone through the trouble of housebreaking. Should the pre-

.vious owner have failed to do so, the responsibility falls on you, and can be executed according to the same method. However, since older dogs tend to have a longer attention span than puppies, you may not have to invest quite so much time in the process.

Paper-Training

Paper-training should not be practiced in tandem with house-breaking, because the two processes have completely opposite goals. Housebreaking aims to impress on your dog the habit of relieving herself exclusively outdoors; paper-training involves teaching her to do the same in a certain area of the house. Any attempt to combine the two will confuse her, and cause a certain amount of justifiable resentment.

You'll have to decide on a spot in the house where your dog will take care of her needs. Cover the area with several layers of newspaper, and lead her to the spot immediately after she eats or drinks, as well as every time you recognize an impulse to eliminate. Just as she would learn to expect a visit to the outdoors, so she will learn to visit her papered area. Bear in mind that she may not perform consistently for the rest of her life. The distinction between one area of the house and another is not nearly as clear as that between inside and outside.

Paper-training best serves the needs of elderly or physically challenged owners, who may not be able to maintain a consistent walking schedule. Young puppies who can't endure severe cold or have not received their full round of vaccinations may also need to be paper-trained for a while. Unfortunately, indoor elimination tends to leave behind an intriguing odor, which only rigorous cleanup will neutralize. Paper-training a large dog, such as a Newfoundland or an Akita, typically involves more work than housebreaking. Male dogs, on the whole, make very poor candidates: By the age of six months they have begun to lift their legs to urinate, and will therefore leave behind nearly ineradicable stains on surfaces and walls.

Schedules

Regularity is the key to happiness, as far as dogs are concerned. They like to be walked first thing in the morning, just before bedtime at night, and after every meal. Not particularly adventuresome in their tastes, they expect the same type of food to show up in their bowls, at regular intervals, every day. Occasional lapses on your part may be forgiven, but persistent fluctuations in schedule are liable to produce anxiety, irritability, and frustration. It's not your dog's fault if you come home to find garbage strewn across the kitchen floor, or an aromatic puddle in the dining room. Though you'll have to reprimand him, the real responsibility for such conduct rests on your shoulders.

Walking

Schedules are typically based on the age and size of your dog. A few general rules may be observed, however:

Your first responsibility every morning is to walk your dog. Naturally, you may need to address certain physical needs of your own before pulling on your coat and boots and heading out into the brisk morning air. You can probably extend the sphere of personal activities to brushing your teeth. But you cannot reasonably expect your dog to sit idly by while you shower, dress, and arrange your hair. If you can't face the world without scrupulous attention to your appearance, consider investing in a long coat, a wide-brimmed hat, and a pair of oversized sunglasses.

Walk your dog promptly after giving food or water. Eating and drinking stimulate the body to divest itself of waste. You have no doubt observed this phenomenon in your own life. There is no reason to assume that your dog's digestive system functions much differently from your own.

Your last duty every night is to walk your dog. Few people savor the idea of waking in the middle of the night to desperate whining or a pleading face hovering by the pillow. You and your dog will sleep more comfortably if you walk him four or five hours after his last drink, as it generally takes this long for water to pass through his system. Food passes through an adult dog's system in roughly ten to twelve hours; six to eight hours in the case of an adolescent; three to five in the case of puppies and small dogs. Once most of the solid and liquid waste has been eliminated, your dog can usually hold what little remains for about eight hours. Accordingly, the time of the last walk will determine your morning wake-up call.

Small dogs must be walked more frequently than large dogs. This point is often lost on less imaginative owners, who expect an adult Chihuahua to master her bodily functions with the same degree of assurance exhibited by a full-grown setter. No amount of discipline can enhance the capacity of a thimble-sized bladder.

Don't deviate from the schedule you establish. Occasional late-night snacks and between-meal samplings may satisfy you, but your dog will come to expect them. This not only complicates his walking schedule, but may lead to obesity. Never offer scraps from the dinner table, as this will not only disrupt his schedule but also encourage begging. Finally, keep toilets covered. Once your dog discovers a ready supply of cool water, he'll drink whenever thirst strikes, and afterward, promptly need to urinate.

Feeding

The amount of food you serve at each meal will depend on your dog's size, age, and activity rate. Obviously, a 180-pound mastiff will not thrive on the same portions you would normally serve a three-pound Pomeranian. When you visit your vet for the first time, ask about weight levels appropriate to each phase of your dog's development. A vet can usually provide you with a growth chart, and advise you concerning the proper portions to feed her to maintain the target weight corresponding to her age and breed.

Younger dogs must be fed more often than older animals. The first year of a puppy's life is characterized by rapid growth and development. Pound for pound, they need more protein and other nutrients to sustain this astonishing biological process. Yet, because their stomachs are small, they can't possibly accommodate their nutritional needs at one feeding. Frequent feedings and specially formulated puppy foods should meet their dietary needs quite handsomely. While food intake tapers off gradually with age, water and walking requirements remain fairly constant.

Typical feeding and walking schedules for dogs at various stages of development include the following:

Two to Three Months Old*

First thing	Morning walk
Upon return	Food, water, and another walk
4 hours later	Food, water, and another walk
4 or 5 hours later	Food, water, and another walk
3 hours later	Food, water, and another walk
3 or 4 hours later	Last walk

*At this stage, some puppies may still need to relieve themselves once or twice during the night.

Three to Six Months Old**

First thing	Morning walk
Upon return	Food, water, and another walk
4 hours later	Food, water, and another walk
4 or 5 hours later	Food, water, and another walk
3 hours later	Water, and another walk
3 or 4 hours later	Last walk

**At this stage, puppies should already be housebroken.

Six Months to One Year Old

First thing	Morning walk
Upon return	Food, water, and another walk
5 hours later	Water and walk, if possible
4 or 5 hours later	Food, water, and walk
3 hours later	Water and walk
3 or 4 hours later	Last walk

One Year and Older

First thing	Morning walk
Upon return	Food, water, and another walk
5 hours later	Water and walk, if possible
4 or 5 hours later	Water and walk
3 hours later	Water and walk
3 or 4 hours later	Last walk

Diet

Dogs are predominantly, but not exclusively, carnivorous. Not even dinosaurs could survive on a diet of meat alone, typically devouring bones, flesh, organic secretions, and any herbaceous matter that lay undigested in the stomachs of their unfortunate victims. Likewise, wild canines usually eat the entire body of their prey, which affords them a balanced mix of protein, vitamins, minerals, carbohydrates, fats, and moisture.

Domestic dogs require the same nutritional balance in order to maintain good health. Many commercially prepared foods supply protein, vitamins, minerals, and so forth in the proper proportions. Others are not balanced and should be offered sparingly, as treats, since they account for part of your dog's total daily intake. Likewise, leftovers or table scraps should account for no more than 15 percent of your dog's daily portion.

Protein, carbohydrates, and fats supply your dog's energy needs. Choose a premium meat- or fish-based dog food that offers between 22 and 26 percent protein and 12 to 15 percent fat for adult dogs. Puppies, pregnant or nursing mothers, extremely active dogs, and dogs who spend most of their time outdoors may need higher percentages of both. Less active dogs may require less. Never add vitamin or mineral supplements unless prescribed by a veterinarian.

Most pet stores and supermarkets offer three basic types of commercial food:

Dry foods are typically composed of dried meat or meat by-products, vegetable protein, cereals, fats, vitamins, and minerals. With only 10 percent moisture content, dry foods keep well. However, an exclusively dry diet may not provide sufficient moisture, even if you set down adequate amounts of water. It's therefore wise to supplement dry food with moist or semimoist portions.

Moist, canned food contains cooked muscle meats, organ meats, fish, carbohydrates, vitamins, and minerals. An exclusively moist diet will not serve your dog's teeth very well, while the attractive taste may gradually incline your pet to overeat. "Scientifically formulated" brands, available through pet stores and veterinarians, generally offer the best nutritional balance; many such brands are formulated to suit the dietary needs of puppies, nursing mothers, and overweight or less active dogs. When buying a commercial, or supermarket, brand, make sure the label states that the product is balanced and complete. Some canned varieties are not complete, and are designed for special pampering or treats. Also, meat and organ meats should be listed ahead of other ingredients, such as meat by-products, to ensure that your dog receives an optimum supply of protein.

Semi-moist foods tend to be high in protein and calories, while providing a balanced supply of other nutrients. Most are composed of meat by-products, soy protein, and cereals. Semi-moist foods contain about 30 to 35 percent water, and do not adequately inhibit tartar buildup, but they can be used to enhance the taste of dry food. Packaging usually consists of airtight pouches, so they can be stored relatively easily. They can be left in the bowl for about twenty-four hours before going stale. Unfortunately, chemicals added to improve flavor and retard spoilage may not be metabolized as readily by dogs as by humans.

Home-cooked meals, if scrupulously prepared according to your veterinarian's recommendations, constitute the best diet you can possibly offer your dog. However, preparing meals from scratch involves time, effort, and concentration. Portion size and composition vary widely according to the size, breed, and activity level of your dog. An unbalanced diet can lead to a number of health problems, ranging from hair loss to pancreatitis. Do not, therefore, try your hand at canine cuisine before consulting your veterinarian.

Chapter 6

Living Together

The first few weeks of owning a dog are often filled with excitement, surprises, and perhaps a few moments of apprehension or regret. As the dust begins to settle, you'll come to realize that you've taken on rather a large commitment. A dog is not a possession: You can't admire him for a while and then tuck him in a closet while you search for something new to satisfy your craving for fulfillment. A dog is here and now, a persistent reminder of the real consequences of your actions.

The first year of your life together will see a number of changes of some sort or another. Obviously, you'll be spending more time outdoors, so your circulation will probably improve and you'll get to see more of your neighbors. Other changes tend to occur on a subtler level, as day after day and week after week, you respond to your dog's most basic needs.

This chapter will explore several aspects of a kind of participation that will gradually redraw your notions of independence and responsibility. These include:

- Training
- Travel
- Grooming
- Breeding
- Veterinary care

Certain issues, such as training and medical care, affect all dog owners. Others, such as grooming, breeding, and travel, vary according to the type of dog adopted, and the intentions and habits of individual owners.

TRAINING

In ancient times, a dog's dinner did not arrange itself neatly in a can or sealed pouch. The enormous amount of energy expended to hunt and kill a balanced meal was usually offset by the size and complexity of the prey. Unfortunately, large animals were difficult to subdue—but a coordinated effort could succeed where individual attempts failed. Dogs who learned to work together survived, whereas those who insisted upon self-reliance were eliminated from the evolutionary equation.

The success of any working group depends on some sort of hierarchy. In this, dogs differ from humankind only in their honesty. Whereas many people pretend to be unaffected by notions of rank, dogs make no attempt to conceal their obsession. Their first impulse upon encountering a stranger is to determine where he or she fits in the scheme of things.

When dogs meet each other for the first time, they typically touch noses and then examine each other's nether regions. Precisely how such behavior establishes rank is unclear. Should any doubt arise from such examination, dogs will adopt a fighting stance, with teeth bared and hackles raised. If neither can agree to accept a lower rank, they will fight until one or the other assumes a submissive posture—rolling on his back and presenting his throat to the victor. In the majority of cases, the higher-ranking dog will accept this as an apology. As a rule, however, terriers would rather kill than suffer any doubt about their prestige.

Students of canine social behavior refer to the highest-ranking dog in any group as alpha dog (alpha being the first letter of the Greek alphabet). Although the rest of the hierarchy remains largely unnamed, a chain of command presumably descends through the pack, terminating at the youngest or most feeble members. Alpha dog determines where the pack will sleep, when they will hunt, who will eat the choicest bits, and other important matters. His authority is rarely questioned, though, as in the case of strangers, any persistent doubts are usually settled by a fight.

Hierarchical perception is a basic element of canine psychology. Puppies instinctively respond to the inquisitive approach of an older, stronger animal by rolling onto their backs and exposing their throats. As they grow older, they make the same inquiries of other dogs, submitting or accepting surrender as the situation demands. For this reason, introduction to human society at an early age is crucial. Puppies who learn to defer to the authority of their human caretakers will usually—unless abused or neglected—accept discipline throughout their lives. Puppies who don't make such a connection will tend to question human authority later on.

Someone must assume the role of alpha dog from the outset, or your dog will assume the duty falls on her shoulders. In households of more than one person, the primary caretaker assumes this role. Other members of the household, though still superior, tend to command somewhat less respect. The only appreciable means to establish dominance is through training. Training begins the minute your dog sets foot in your house for the first time. Naturally, you will need to be rather gentle with a puppy in the beginning. Your primary concerns will consist of protecting her from danger and inhibiting the formation of undesirable habits. Should you decide to train your dog on your own, it is recommended that you study one or more of the excellent training videos currently available.

If your puppy has been properly imprinted, she will be primed to accept you as alpha dog. Yet even older dogs can be successfully trained. In some cases, the greater part of training will consist of establishing and reinforcing limitations to compensate for bad habits that have already been allowed to take root. If problem behaviors persist (particularly in the case of large dogs), or if you want to show your dog, you'll probably need the help of a professional trainer. Professional options will be discussed at the end of this section.

Together, a willing dog and a patient owner can devise a number of highly specific routines. Most owners, however, don't require their pets to carry trays, jump through flaming hoops, or sniff out contraband. A basic program will usually suffice, the elements of which lay the foundation for more sophisticated maneuvers. These elements include:

- Trust
- Tools
- Voice and body language
- Rewards
- Reprimands
- Consistency

Since training takes place on a variety of levels, all these elements come into play in some form or another. Physical control by itself will not suffice, nor can you expect your dog to simply intuit your wishes. Without consistent reinforcement, acquired skills are apt to fade rather quickly from memory.

Trust

Trust is the cornerstone of successful training. Your dog must have confidence in your ability to command. Such faith results, in large part, from your approach to training. If you observe a mother dog teaching her young, you'll notice her firm but gentle manner. She remains focused on the lesson at hand, and refrains from calling heaven to witness the stubbornness or stupidity of her child. She rewards success promptly, and delivers reprimands without fuss. A nip, a swat, or a quick shake is enough to tell puppy his behavior is unacceptable.

Early training sessions should last no more than ten minutes. Very young puppies, due to a limited attention span, may grow restless or bored after five. After a couple of weeks of daily practice, you can gradually increase lesson time. By the end of six weeks of training, lessons may continue comfortably for twenty or thirty minutes. Beyond half an hour, however, both you and your dog will probably begin to show signs of stress. End the lesson well before you've reached the limit of your patience. Above all, you must have confidence in yourself. If you've never been in a position to command, you will need to develop this capacity. In this sense, a dog functions as master teacher of the old style, whose willingness to trust her students awakens their thirst to learn. This trust eventually becomes reciprocal: As your faith in your ability to command increases, so will your confidence in your dog's ability to respond. The real goal of training is not to induce your dog to execute your instructions by rote, but rather to establish a rapport or sympathy on which you both can depend in a variety of unpredictable situations.

Tools

The basic tools of training include:

Training Leash. A six-foot leash allows your dog some freedom of movement, while still affording you ample control. Leather works best, although some owners prefer nylon or canvas. For training purposes, don't use anything fancy or decorative.

Corrective Collar. Often referred to as a "choke collar" or "choke chain," because a slight tug on the leash applies pressure to the neck. Make sure you receive instructions in the correct manner of putting on a correcting collar. More importantly, it should never be used to actually choke a dog, merely to apply a brief tug. A chain-link collar is best suited for large or stubborn animals; small- or medium-sized links are preferred, as large ones may become tangled. However, puppies, small or placid dogs, and dogs with long hair should only wear nylon or leather collars. Whatever material you use, make sure the collar is three inches longer than the circumference of your dog's neck.

As mentioned in Chapter Five, the Promise head collar is viewed by many as a more humane alternative to a metal corrective collar. The Promise is a sort of hybrid harness and muzzle; the leash attaches under the dog's chin. The Promise offers control of the dog's entire head, rather than his neck and shoulders. It works extremely well with aggressive or hyperactive dogs.

Throw chain. The noise of a tossed chain can startle your dog, directing her attention away from whatever may have distracted her and back to you. A device of this kind can be made by tying a few knots in a spare chain-link collar. In conjunction with the word "No," a throw chain serves to associate your command with an unpleasant experience. Never throw the chain directly at or near your dog; if you frighten or injure your dog you will undo all the effects of training. Instead, toss the chain behind your body or at your side.

Shake Can. As an alternative to a throw chain, you can fill an empty soda can with pebbles or coins, and shake it behind you, at your side, or above your head. Never use a glass container, and don't toss the can at your dog or shake it in her direction; again, you merely want to get her attention, not scare the daylights out of her. Shy or nervous dogs may find the noise of a shake can too upsetting; in such cases, you're better using a throw chain.

As a general note, if you're about to embark on the adventure of training a puppy, let her get used to her collar and leash well before lessons commence. Allow her to spend a day or two sniffing and pawing at these strange-looking implements; make a game of slipping on the collar and attaching the leash, and let her meander around the house while you keep only a light grip on the leash. If you play this game a few times before venturing outdoors, chances are she'll offer less resistance when training begins. Where possible, it's best to begin outside work in a quiet area, gradually introducing her to busier sidewalks as her discipline and confidence increase.

Voice

Your dog's ears are far more sensitive than your own. Her ability to perceive subtleties in pitch and tone comes from her wild ancestors, for whom the difference between a falling leaf and the stealthy tread of a downwind predator figured quite significantly. Even among modern dogs, certain types of sounds provoke immediate reactions. Loud or sharp noises, for example, command attention, while deep, growling tones tend to trigger an aggressive response.

By the time puppies begin exploring their surroundings, they can usually distinguish between the different vocal patterns their mothers use to express contentment, encouragement, warning, and reproach. Human caretakers typically use words or other vocalizations to reinforce these basic signals. Just by spending time around people, dogs learn many of the nuances of the human voice. Consequently, the way you speak to your dog will convey as much, if not more, than the actual commands you give.

Whether you're aware of it or not, your voice tends to reflect your mood. For this reason, it's best to begin each training session in a calm, undistracted frame of mind. Such states are relative, of course. Suffice it to say that you should probably not begin a session immediately after receiving a subpoena.

A few additional guidelines can help make the training process more satisfying for you and your dog:

Tone. Enthusiasm begets enthusiasm. Your dog is much more likely to come, fetch, or go for a walk if you can muster up some excitement about the task. Timid or excitable dogs, however, respond more adeptly to a calm, soothing delivery. The same holds true for dogs faced with an unfamiliar, or otherwise stressful, situation.

Inflection. Match your inflection to the nature of the command. A steady, level inflection best serves commands such as "Sit," "Stay," or "Heel," where the desired behavior is relatively calm or controlled. Use a downward inflection when commanding your dog to lay down; an upward accent when you want her to run or fetch.

"**No.**" For the sake of clarity, this is the only word of reprimand you should ever use. For maximum effectiveness, speak it distinctly and emphatically; don't drag out the syllable or inflect it in any way. Avoid bellowing, too, unless you must communicate across a great distance. Should you allow panic or anger to affect your tone, or follow up with condemnatory or abusive language, you undercut the power of this useful command entirely.

Brevity. Keep commands concise. Faulknerian phrases, like "Go to that corner and use your teeth to pick up the small red rubber ball and bring it back to where I'm standing and drop it at my feet and repeat the whole process when I throw the ball again because you're a good dog who always does what I tell you" supply far more information than your dog can reasonably associate with an activity. "Fetch" gets the point across more vividly, and may be used in a wide variety of circumstances.

Name. Always use an encouraging or affectionate tone when speaking your dog's name, so she will form a positive association. *Never, never, never* speak her name harshly or in connection with any sort of reprimand. The temptation to do so is very great, but the effect on your dog can range from confusion to suspicion or distrust.

Body Language

Like your voice, your body conveys a number of distinct signals, some intentional and some less so. Accordingly, you need to exercise the same care when handling your dog as you would while speaking to her. Your hands, for example, should be used solely to express affection or encouragement. If Priscilla associates your hands with undeniably pleasant activities such as patting, brushing, or stroking, she is less likely to take offense when you manually position her during your first few lessons in sitting and lying down.

Fortunately, in all lessons involving the leash, your hands remain out of the line of sight. Since leash-training involves an occasional tug of the collar, your dog is free to assume that the leash—not your hands—delivered the reprimand. Even so, you must guard against using excessive force in all dealings with your dog. A gentle tug of the leash will suffice to correct a small dog or a puppy. While larger dogs require somewhat stronger measures, you may inflict pain if you pull too hard. Pain of any sort creates a climate of distrust, which will invalidate everything your dog has learned so far.

Similarly, abrupt or threatening gestures tend to inspire fear rather than respect. If you stand glowering over your dog, shaking your finger or fist, you run the risk of an aggressive response. In her wisdom, she may understand that you are physically stronger; instead of expressing herself directly, she'll find some other means to get back at you—perhaps by running away, marking your car, or burying your stamp collection in the rose garden. Even worse, she'll be right.

Rewards

Very few creatures perform a task without some expectation of reward. Sometimes the reward consists of avoiding unpleasantness. More often, it takes the form of something quite positive or enjoyable. From time to time, of course, nobler motives can inspire selfless action; but an honest appraisal of habitual behavior will likely rate such moments exceptional. There is no reason to expect your dog to respond to training in a manner contrary to the norm.

Rewards of both a verbal and an edible variety typically motivate a dog to perform. In the beginning, the two should be offered simultaneously: Praise your dog and give him a lovely biscuit when he completes a task. Even if you have to mold his body physically—as you almost certainly will when teaching a new command—reward him as soon as he's in position. Immediate compensation forges a link between his physical posture, the biscuit, and your cheerful words of praise. Over time, you may reduce the number of biscuits in exchange for more liberal helpings of praise.

In fact, applied with genuine enthusiasm, praise is the most effective training tool in your kit. Precisely how a dog can distinguish between false expressions of delight and honest approval remains a closely guarded secret. Odors undetectable to the human nostril probably play a decisive role. In any case, your dog's ability to learn often varies directly in proportion to the pleasure you take in her response.

Reprimands

Like rewards, reprimands work best when administered promptly. There's no point in reprimanding your dog for something that happened hours before you arrived on the scene. He simply won't remember doing it; as far as he knows, there's always been a hole in the piano. However, if you can stop your dog in the middle of an act you want to discourage, a causal connection is established.

The aim of any type of reprimand is to startle your dog, not to punish him. You want the *activity itself* to seem unpleasant, rather than your response to it. A loud, sharp "No," a tossed chain, or the rattling of a shake can is usually enough of a jolt to link the physical sensations of a racing heart and a burst of adrenaline with whatever behavior he was engaged in at the moment. Where such measures fail, you might consider a quick blast from a water pistol, or a loud whistle. Certain desperate situations may require a swat on the nose or rump with a rolled-up magazine or the brush end of a broom—using just enough force to surprise, not cause pain. At all costs, avoid showing anger or frustration. As easily as your dog associates your praise with warm, pleasant feelings, he'll come to fear your anger as a threat.

Consistency

Training is an extremely intimate activity. As with anything that involves a fair amount of subtle communication, skillful timing, and pleasurable stroking, it is best performed in private. Choose a quiet room or section of the backyard, where you and your dog can focus on the lesson at hand. Opportunities for distraction will inevitably present themselves if you attempt to train her in the front yard or sidewalk. Just as Queenie's about to grasp the intricacies of the "Sit" command, someone is liable to run up to tell you how sweet she looks—or worse, to offer advice.

Your dog will learn faster if you bring her to the same spot each time you teach a new command. Canine memory is holographic: smells, sounds, or familiar sights trigger complex physical reactions that set in motion patterns of behavior associated with a specific experience. If Queenie associates her training area with praise and treats, chances are she'll return there all the more eagerly—and respond more quickly to your commands—because she knows what's coming. After she's mastered each command in the training area, you can gradually extend practice into more distracting environments.

Discouraging undesirable behavior also requires consistency. If, for example, you want to keep your dog from begging at the dinner table, you will have to shake a can or say "No!" every time she approaches, until she concedes the point. Visitors and young children may fail to grasp the importance of consistency; and you may occasionally find yourself too tired or preoccupied to enforce the rules you've laid down. Unfortunately, a single lapse will teach your dog that she can sometimes get away with bad behavior. While vigilance in this regard may seem to demand too much effort, your dog will conform far more quickly if you stand firm from the outset.

What Every Dog Should Know

You must be able to control your dog's behavior in a variety of circumstances, both at home and out in the world. Failure to establish certain basic command patterns puts you, your dog—and everything else between—in grave danger. Moreover, an ill-behaved dog easily becomes a nuisance. You risk bringing the wrath of your neighbors upon your head if you refuse to teach your dog a few basic rules of deportment.

Aside from the all-important "No," a well-behaved dog will understand at least the following commands:

Sit. This command is used to control your dog's excitement or curiosity in a variety of situations. It can be used effectively when stopping to chat in the middle of a walk or entering a crowded elevator, or if visitors find your dog's attentions a bit unnerving. Teach this command while holding your dog on a short leash, so he must hold his head erect. As you say the word "Sit," press down on his rear end until he is resting on his haunches. Promptly tell him what a good boy he is and give him a cookie. Repeat this until he sits on his own at your command, immediately after which you must tell him he's a *wonderful* boy and give him two cookies. As he becomes more confident, you can cut back on the cookies, until you're satisfied he'll accept a pat on the head and a gentle word of praise.

Down or Lie Down. If your dog is making a general nuisance of himself—for instance, nosing among guests at a cocktail party or interrupting private conversations—you can put an end to his intrusions by commanding him to lie down. As with the "Sit" command, keep him on a short leash. As you say "Lie down," push on his rump and neck until he complies. If your dog is large, try sliding or gently pulling his front legs forward as you press down on his backside. If he attempts to rise immediately, repeat the command firmly while holding him in place. Offer praise and cookies as before, until he has mastered the command. "Lie down" can be used in combination with "Come" or "Stay," as described below.

Heel. The essential walking command, "Heel" is used to keep your dog by your side. You particularly need firm control when walking a large breed or guard dog, when approaching a strange animal, or walking down busy streets or crowded areas. Begin training with a short leash in a quiet area. Don't hold the leash too tightly, or your dog will inevitably pull, blurring the distinction between normal walking and heeling. Keep talking as you walk, to hold his attention.

As you command "Heel," gently but firmly tug on the leash until his head is in line with your leg. Follow with praise, but no cookies, as pausing to consume a treat will interrupt the smooth flow of practice. Keep early practice sessions short to avoid taxing your dog's patience; if he strains at the leash, command him to sit, and resume the lesson after a brief pause.

Stay. Like a red stoplight, this command tells your dog to maintain whatever position he's in. It's extremely useful at busy intersections or when you require him to sit or lie down for an extended period. (Short-legged dogs find it hard to sit for any length of time.) You can teach "Stay" at the same time you teach "Sit" and "Lie down." Once your dog has assumed or been placed in the proper position, hold your palm about five inches in front of his eyes so that it's the only thing he sees. When he tries to move, tell him to "Stay" while tugging on the leash; in this way, he'll associate the command with the palm of your hand and the sensation of restraint. Reward with praise and cookies.

Gradually increase the distance between you and your dog as you drill the command, until you reach the end of the leash. At this point, you can begin training him to stay while you remove yourself to another room. "Stay" can be practiced while walking by giving the command while pulling hard enough on the leash to inhibit movement. You may need to place a hand under your dog's belly to keep him from assuming a sitting position.

Okay. Like "No," this is a universal command—to be used when you release your dog from staying, sitting, lying down. "Okay" needs relatively little practice: Back away, tug on the leash slightly, and offer a treat as you say the magic word.

Come. This crucial command is used to call your dog to your side when he is off-leash, or to release him from sitting or lying down. Its power disintegrates, however, if you once use the command to summon your dog for reprimand or correction; you must go to him when he's done something inappropriate. ''Come'' is most effective when used in conjunction with your dog's name. Begin practice by placing your dog in a sitting or lying position, and then release him, saying ''Okay, Scylla—come.'' Give a slight tug on the leash, and repeat ''Come'' or ''Come here, boy'' in an encouraging voice while slowly pulling the leash toward you.

Avoid dragging your dog: If necessary, tempt him with a biscuit. When he's directly in front of you, command him to sit or lie down, give him the biscuit and lay on the praise. Repeat this until he comes to you on command, then gradually increase the distance he must travel by walking backward as you continue to call him. The final stage of practice, in which you drop the leash before calling him to you, must be practiced indoors or in an enclosed yard until you are absolutely sure he will come when called. Gradually introduce distractions into the practice area before attempting to carry the lesson into the real world.

Professional Options

If you quail at the thought of training your dog on your own, you might want to engage a professional trainer. Trainers can also serve to resolve behavioral problems, or to give specialized training for dog shows, guiding, guarding, and a host of other useful activities. Professional training falls under three broad categories:

Private lessons are usually conducted in your home, or occasionally at the trainer's studio or classroom. The trainer works closely with you and your dog to instill basic commands, or resolve problems. As with most forms of private training, this option can be expensive.

Classroom training will accustom your dog to dealing with other dogs and strangers, and can therefore minimize aggressive tendencies. Group lessons are typically less expensive than other options. However, you must make attendance a high priority; if you miss a class, you and your dog will fall behind very quickly.

Kennel training involves boarding your dog at a kennel for a period of two weeks or longer, where, like a West Point cadet, he'll undergo an intensive training procedure. At the end of training, you must arrange subsequent sessions in your own home. You must learn to command your dog as he's been taught, or else he won't respond.

To locate a reliable trainer of the sort you wish to engage, consult your veterinarian, a reputable breeder, or your local dog club or ASPCA. You can also solicit advice from owners whose dogs behave impeccably. In addition, a number of dog clubs hold regular group sessions for dogs who have completed a course in basic obedience.

PROBLEM BEHAVIORS

The most common problems that confront a dog owner are house soiling, chewing or shredding, and aggression. In most cases, prevention involves far less work than correction. The first order of business is to determine the underlying cause of problem behavior. If you merely attempt to correct the symptom, you'll find yourself caught up in a perpetual cycle of hope and frustration.

Soiling

A medical problem may underlie persistent house soiling. Dogs infested with internal parasites, for example, can't control their bowels with the same degree of accuracy as uninfested dogs. Females, meanwhile, sometimes suffer from low-grade infections of the urinary tract, which can account for occasional, accidental wetting. Before attempting to correct behavior of this kind, consult your veterinarian.

Bear in mind, too, males reach sexual maturity at around seven or eight months. At this point, they begin lifting their legs to spray urine as a means of marking their territory and calling attention to themselves. It is the canine equivalent of burning rubber or spray-painting one's initials on a water tower or overpass. The only effective way to prevent spraying is to neuter your dog. Neutering offers a number of other advantages, which will be discussed later in this chapter.

If the problem has no medical or sexual basis, your dog may simply not have sufficient access to the outdoors. Try adding another walk to her schedule, or increase the time you spend together outside, to ensure she has ample opportunity to relieve herself. You must also neutralize the scent in any soiled area, or it will call your dog to visit again and again; a number of commercial products have been expressly designed for this purpose.

Lead your dog to the spot once it is clean and dry, and make her lie there for a while. Dogs generally don't like to soil areas where they know they'll be spending a good deal of time: Urine and feces are traditionally used to mark the outer limits of their territory—that is, areas most likely to be probed by other animals. Likewise, if your dog soils the house while you're away, try keeping her in her crate or use a gate to confine her to the room where she eats or sleeps.

Destructiveness

House soiling, chewing, and shredding are often caused by anxiety. Dogs often get nervous when they don't know when, or if, their owners will return. In an attempt to soothe their shattered nerves, they chew a pillow or shred a throw rug—which produces the same effect as eating a piece of chocolate cake or a bowl of ice cream might have on you. You can minimize anxiety by gradually conditioning your dog to accept your absence. Start by leaving your dog alone for only a few minutes at a time, and work your way up to longer and longer intervals. At the same time, don't make a production of every greeting and farewell. If you keep them brief and calm, your dog won't assume each leave-taking is a momentous occasion.

On the other hand, chewing and shredding may simply stem from lack of exercise or other suitable stimulation. Make sure your dog has sufficient time outdoors to burn off excess energy. A ten-minute walk three times a day is roughly equal to getting out of your office chair and sitting immediately back down; before too long, you'd go a little stir-crazy yourself. By nature, dogs need to chew, and should be provided with appropriate objects. Never make toys out of castoff clothes or footwear, or your entire wardrobe becomes fair game. At the same time, if you provide your dog with too many toys, at some point she'll begin to think everything on the floor is hers by right.

Should you catch your dog playing with something unsuitable, don't wrestle it out of her mouth or paws. She'll think you're playing a game with her. The preferred method involves distracting her with an appropriate toy. Pour praise on her when she comes to get it from you, and while she's occupied with this new object, quietly remove her former obsession from the area.

Dogs can also indulge in destructive habits because you're not around to discourage them. If Maggie routinely devours your beeswax candles or attacks your stuffed animals, you'll need a reprimand system that can function in your absence. One successful method involves attaching a shake can to the favored object and concealing the can from view. As your dog grasps or dislodges the object, the shake can clatters to the ground.

Chewing stationary objects requires a somewhat different approach. If your dog develops a habit of chewing electrical cords, personal items, or decorative objects, try spraying the surface with Bitter Apple, which has a foul taste by any standard. Bitter Apple will mar the finish on wooden surfaces, however. Instead, treat chair legs, end tables, and so forth with a sour paste made of alum and water.

Aggression

The most common causes of hyperaggressive behavior include prior abuse, inadequate socialization, and incompetent training. Of these three, the fruits of incompetence are usually easiest to rectify—though a considerable amount of effort may still be required. Aggressive behavior of this sort occurs because no one in the household has assumed the role of alpha dog. Like a child thrust into an adult role, a dog assumes an enormous amount of stress along with the mantle of power.

Naturally, the best way to avoid such a situation is to establish your authority from the beginning; however, if you (or a previous owner) ignored this crucial aspect of ownership, rest assured that dogs of any age can learn to obey simple commands. You'll likely meet with some resistance at first, but a consistent schedule of positive training, combined with immediate correction of inappropriate behavior, will eventually convince your dog of your ability to lead.

Likewise, dogs that have had little or no exposure to people and other animals—particularly during the first four months of life—will tend to regard most sounds, smells, and moving objects as potential threats. Enrolling your dog in a group obedience class is often the best means of compensating for inadequate socialization. Not only will she associate with other dogs and people, but you and she will both have a chance to refine obedience skills under the guidance of a professional.

In cases of extreme aggression—or if a large dog shows aggressive tendencies—you may need to engage a private instructor before enrolling in a group class. At home, you can help to diffuse anxiety when the doorbell rings by reprimanding your dog for excessive barking, and by greeting visitors with the same tone of voice you use when praising your dog. Visitors may question your sanity, but they will usually prefer a bit of chirping over a nasty bite on the leg.

If your dog was abused by a previous owner, or if you suspect such abuse occurred, you may not be able to curb her aggressive tendencies. Consult your veterinarian first; in some cases, he or she may be able to prescribe medical or holistic treatment to calm your dog. On no account should you medicate your dog without veterinary authorization. A dog's metabolism is calibrated very differently from your own. If your vet feels the dog's aggressive tendencies can be resolved, he or she may be able to recommend a trainer. If the problem appears irreversible, the kindest solution may be to release the animal from the trials of this world.

TRAVEL

By now it should be clear that most dogs can't be left alone for extended periods. If your regular schedule involves being away from home more than eight or nine hours at a time, you should consider hiring someone to walk your dog during the day; chances are, when you return home, you won't have the energy to endure an hour or two in the park.

Unlike most other types of pets, dogs can't be left alone for more than ten hours at a stretch. In the very least, they need to relieve themselves. Should your dog break housetraining because you left town without providing for her, you've essentially given her permission to use the living room carpet whenever the need arises. Further, your absence will inspire anxiety or restlessness, opening the door to destructive behavior.

If you're going to be away overnight or longer, you absolutely must make provisions for your dog. Your options include:

- Arranging a sitter
- Engaging someone to provide food and water, and to walk her at least three times a day
- Boarding her
- Taking her along for the trip

Failure to arrange care in your absence is abuse. At best, an unattended dog will make a hash of her surroundings; at worst, she may accidentally injure or kill herself.

Taking Your Dog with You

Most dogs are intrepid voyagers, especially if accustomed to traveling at a young age. Yet many older, less experienced dogs can learn to enjoy travel. The natural curiosity and courage of the canine species enables most dogs to adjust to new surroundings fairly easily.

Whether traveling in your native land or abroad, you will need to investigate any restrictions or regulations particular to your destination. For example, every state in the United States enforces its own guidelines for admitting dogs, so you will have to contact the state legislature or department of agriculture. Many Caribbean islands do not admit dogs at all; Hawaii and Great Britain impose lengthy quarantines. Before setting off for an international adventure or island escape, check with your veterinarian, the airline, or cruise line you're using, or the embassy or travel information bureau of the place you intend to visit.

You'll also need to gather the following materials prior to departure:

- A carrier or cage
- Newspaper or a towel to line the carrier
- Paper towels to clean up accidents
- A certificate of health, signed by your veterinarian
- Proof of rabies inoculation
- Medications your dog regularly requires
- A first-aid kit
- Moist and dry food
- A bottle of water
- A can opener and spoon
- Food bowls
- Grooming tools

If your dog does not regularly sleep in his carrier or cage, place it out in the open a few days before the trip, so your dog can explore it. Especially if he's a seasoned traveler, this will help to prepare him to expect a trip. On the day of departure, make sure the crate or carrier is lined with newspaper. Spend a little extra cozy time together, if possible, but don't feed him ten hours before departure (five hours, if he's a puppy). This should give him time to digest his food and empty his bowels.

You may wish to ask your veterinarian about tranquilizers. Your dog probably won't need them, as most do not enjoy sedation. *Never give your dog tranquilizers prescribed for humans.* Only give medications that have been authorized by a veterinarian, and only in the dosage prescribed.

Traveling by Car

Chances are, your dog has already ridden with you on several occasions and is accustomed to traveling without a cage or carrier. If this is not the case, and if time allows, take him for rides of increasing length before your vacation together. This will give him the chance to find his balance and allow you to ascertain whether or not you can drive safely with Pompey loose in the car. Whether taking a trip across town or across the country, a dog's proper place is the backseat, where he is less likely to interfere with your driving or fly through the windshield in case of an accident.

If you plan on stopping along the way, make sure in advance that the motel or hotel allows pets. Many campgrounds allow dogs, although certain rules must be observed, so it's wise to contact the management before arrival. Never leave your dog in the car. No doubt, you will notice a number of foolish people fail to observe this rule; it is one of the best arguments for resurrecting the honorable practice of public humiliation in the stocks. When the sun is shining, the temperature inside a vehicle can climb to 120 degrees in a matter of minutes, and your dog can suffer heatstroke. By the same token, on a cold day, the temperature inside the vehicle will rapidly drop, and your dog may freeze.

Public Transportation

Many public carriers will allow dogs, if they are suitably contained. Amtrak, however, expressly prohibits pets; as do many interstate bus lines. Cruise ships rarely allow dogs, and those that do may insist that they travel in special kennel areas. Most airlines allow canine passengers; all require advance registration, however, which typically involves a fee. In addition, most require health certificates and proof of rabies inoculation, so you will need to visit your veterinarian well beforehand.

Airlines are usually quite particular about the dimensions of the carrier or kennel. Small dogs may be allowed to travel in the passenger section of the plane, provided the carrier fits under the seat. Large dogs will be transported in the cargo section. The U.S. Department of Agriculture and the Civil Aeronautics Board have established strict temperature and air quality guidelines for areas in which animals are contained during flight. Age and health regulations have also been enacted, as follows:

- Puppies less than eight weeks old are not allowed on board.
- If puppies between eight and sixteen weeks will travel longer than twelve hours at a stretch, owners must provide food, water, and feeding instructions.
- Older dogs traveling up to twenty-four hours or longer must be provided with the same. Since not all airlines are required to administer food and water in flight, however, you must check with your carrier before making reservations for a long trip.
- Health certificates and/or proof of rabies inoculation may be required by the airline, the state veterinary officials, or both. Consult your veterinarian about the type of certification required.
- Dogs traveling without their owners may not be left at the terminal more than four hours before departure. Exceptions may be offered at terminals equipped with a kennel facility or animalport.
- Carriers or kennels must comply with strict standards for durability, ventilation, sanitation, and size. In general, carriers must be large enough for the dog to stand fully upright and to turn around normally; exceptions apply to racing dogs, such as greyhounds and whippets, who may suffer spinal damage if allowed to turn around in cramped quarters. The carrier must be fitted with handles so transporters can lift it in an upright position.

In addition to complying with these guidelines, you should also attach the following to the outside of the carrier or kennel:

- A sign announcing the carrier contains a live animal
- Your dog's name
- Your name, address, and telephone number
- Feeding instructions
- Pertinent medical information

- A supply of any medications your dog regularly requires

Airline travel can be hard on a dog, especially during trips of five hours or more. Not only is your dog likely to go a little stir-crazy if confined for a long period, the noise levels in the cargo section may upset him or possibly damage his ears. Pekingese, pugs, bulldogs, and other short-nosed dogs are prone to breathing problems, and may suffocate in cargo compartments, where the air is usually quite thin. Accordingly, air travel should be kept to a minimum, and undertaken only after consulting your veterinarian.

Leaving Your Dog Home

For short trips of less than a week, many people prefer to arrange for someone to walk, feed, and spend a bit of time with their dogs. Depending on your location, a number of professional walking services may be available. Since the operators will have access to your home, and will be responsible for your dog's health and welfare in your absence, you should probably consult your veterinarian or a trusted pet store manager for the name of a service known for its reliability. Friends or coworkers may also be able to recommend reliable walkers, or may be persuaded to care for your dog themselves.

An alternative to engaging a professional service is to arrange for a friend or family member to stay with your dog. The sitter should have some experience in handling and living with a dog. An inexperienced sitter may inadvertently leave a door or window open, or may not be able to manage confrontations with other dogs or other such crises.

Whichever option you choose, you must arrange for the sitter or walker to meet with you and your dog prior to your departure. This will ensure your dog does not mistake his caretaker for an intruder, and will also give you an opportunity to observe the caretaker's interaction with your pet. You'll also need to discuss instructions on care and feeding, and provide the caretaker with telephone numbers where you can be reached, as well as the phone number and address of your veterinarian.

Boarding

When circumstances don't permit traveling with your dog—and if you can't or don't feel comfortable arranging for someone to

visit three or more times a day—you must provide for care outside your home. Ideally, this will mean boarding her with a friend
or family member who knows her and would enjoy looking after
a temporary companion. If this person has dogs or cats, you
should arrange a visit in advance of your departure to make sure
the animals will get along.

Of course, the ideal situation doesn't always present itself, so
you may need to board your dog at a kennel. Though tales of
horror surround kennel boarding, most facilities are operated by
reliable souls. In fact, many veterinarians provide kennel services
in their offices or clinics. Still, a stay of any length in an unfamiliar environment, deprived of beloved friends and surrounded
by strange dogs, can give rise to anxious feelings and behavior.
Your dog may become aggressive, surly, or ill while boarded.

Accordingly, you should make every effort to choose the most
scrupulously operated facility you can find. Consult your veterinarian and ask friends and acquaintances who own animals. You
may also consult the breeder from whom you acquired your dog;
in some cases, breeders will temporarily board dogs they know.
Once you've collected a list of possibilities, visit each one, and
evaluate them according to the following factors:

- Cleanliness
- Attitude of caregivers
- Temperature
- Physical and emotional well-being of animals
- Diet
- Number and length of daily exercise periods
- Size of exercise area (dog runs should be at least twenty
  feet long)

You'll also need to find out if the management requires a
health certificate and proof of rabies inoculation prior to boarding.
Make sure your dog is current on all vaccinations, even if proof
is not required. This will minimize the risk of contracting an infectious disease.

Provide the operators of the facility with emergency contact
information—including your telephone numbers, your vet's, and
a friend's or relative's who can act on your behalf should the
need arise. If allowed, bring along some of your dog's toys, and
an article or two of your clothing she can sleep with. When you

pick her up, make sure you have a box or can of her favorite treats handy.

Moving

If your dog is used to being left or boarded when you are away, preparations for a move can cause anxiety. She may feel that she's going to be left behind. Be considerate, therefore, and speak to her reassuringly as you allow her to investigate the packing boxes. Above all, be sure to compensate for any shortness of temper by spending extra time with your dog. You'll probably benefit, as well, from spending time outdoors.

Moving day is often noisy and confusing, however, and if you've hired movers, your dog may justifiably greet these strangers with some dismay or suspicion. Unpleasant scenes can usually be avoided by confining your dog to the backyard or an empty room, along with her food and water dishes and a few toys. If this proves impractical, confine her to her crate or carrier in an area least accessible to traffic.

Once the move is complete, place her in a room along with her bed, dishes, and toys; or at the very least, confine her to an area where she is least likely to be disturbed. Arrange your schedule to allow some time together, just as you did when you first brought her home. You may wish to confine her to a single room or area of the home while you're unpacking and organizing your possessions. Once the dust has settled, let her explore her new territory room by room. She may have an accident or two during the period of adjustment. This will likely result from stress—your own and hers. You can help prevent such unpleasant occasions by ensuring she has plenty of exercise outdoors.

GROOMING

Dogs are clean animals who spend a good deal of time outdoors, which is usually less clean than the average dog or the average home. Accordingly, you will need to establish a daily grooming habit, along with more specific weekly and monthly rituals. Grooming is particularly important in the winter months, when dogs tramp through snow, slush, and puddles. In areas where salt is laid, your dog will probably pick up a great deal on his paws or on the fringe of long coats. Salt can damage the paws, and if he ingests too much while licking himself after a walk, he can suffer gastrointestinal discomfort. It's somewhat easier to steer clear of puddles of water, antifreeze, or other chemical agents; still, it's wise to wipe his paws with a wet cloth if you suspect contamination of this sort.

A dog's coat serves as protection against a variety of environmental elements—including water, snow, cold, and heat. Excessive bathing, clipping, or trimming can damage both the coat and the skin. It's important, therefore, to ask your veterinarian during the initial exam about proper grooming techniques. If you acquire your dog from a breeder, ask about bathing, combing, and trimming, and get the name of a reliable professional groomer. The breeder may also be able to recommend a grooming video.

Regular combing and brushing will minimize shedding, keep the coat free of dirt and other sordid particles, and remove fleas, ticks, and other parasites. Grooming also stimulates oil glands at the base of every hair. Tiny oil secretions protect the fur from water and other substances, and give the coat a glossy appearance. Finally, regular grooming sessions provide wonderful opportunities for bonding with your pet.

Dogs groom themselves daily, of course, but optimum maintenance requires your assistance. Long-haired dogs in particular need daily work, because their fur easily becomes tangled and matted. Yet even short-haired dogs need brushing and combing, a bit of nail trimming, a regular inspection of teeth, eyes, and ears, and an occasional bath. The time you must devote to grooming depends on the type of coat your dog has and the degree of comfort you feel regarding certain routines such as trimming nails and bathing.

In some instances, you may want to bring your dog to a professional groomer. Even if you intend to groom him at home, you'll probably want to have him groomed professionally at least once to establish a guideline for his optimum appearance. You can also use the opportunity to ask questions about daily and weekly grooming, as well as purchase grooming tools, shampoos, and other beauty aids. Regular professional treatment is recommended for clipped coats, wiry coats, long coats, unusual coats, and dogs who fidget excessively during long grooming sessions. You can usually minimize the time and expense of regular visits by attending to your dog's daily and weekly grooming needs.

Whether you groom your dog at home or professionally, you need to establish a routine while he's young. Puppies groomed from the time they're weaned generally have little trouble accepting regular attention. In addition, you'll want to groom him in a specific area every time. A table or desktop of average height will usually serve; cover the surface with a rubber mat to provide enough traction for your dog to feel secure. It's a good idea to cover the floor with newspaper or a cloth as well.

General Procedures

Regardless of size, shape, and coat length, all dogs benefit from the following basic procedures:

- Run your hands over his coat and remove burrs, twigs, clumps of dirt, and other unsavory objects. Check for lumps, sores, or other irregularities that may require veterinary attention.
- Dry skin is prone to sores and itching. During the winter months, indoor dogs are especially likely to develop dry skin. Ask your veterinarian if you can add a bit of vegetable oil to your dog's food if you notice flaking or itching.
- Smooth tangles or mats with your fingers. Troublesome tangles may have to be cut away; it's best to have a professional accomplish this delicate task, at least in the beginning.
- Remove ticks as described below in the section dealing with parasites.
- After brushing and combing, use a thin-toothed flea comb to remove adult fleas. Consult your veterinarian about flea sprays, powders, or shampoos. You will need to follow up by spraying or powdering all surfaces where the dog regularly sits or sleeps.
- Use a clean, lint-free cloth to remove plugs of dried mucus from the corners of eyes. Poodles and certain other breeds tear a good deal, so you'll want to wipe deposits from the areas just under the eyes. You can inhibit staining by applying a thin layer of petroleum jelly just under the eye. Consult your veterinarian before doing so, however. Persistent tearing or discharge, redness, or cloudiness may signal a serious condition, which will require veterinary attention. It may turn out to be as simple as a fleck of dirt or an eyelash trapped under the lid; but a dog's eyes are extremely delicate, and most dogs will not hold still while you try to re-

move an offending particle. Even if you can see what's bothering him, you're better off taking your pet to the veterinarian.

- Check ears for dirt, wax, and parasites—particularly in the ear flaps. Long-eared dogs are especially prone to collect dirt and dust, and ears should be checked every other day. Use extreme caution, though, since the ear mechanism can be easily damaged. If necessary, wipe away excess dirt or wax with a cotton ball dipped in lukewarm, soapy water. Do not use swabs designed for human use. Parasites may be removed with tweezers only if your dog does not fidget; otherwise, a professional should attend to them. Redness, swelling, or discharge in the ear signals the presence of an infection. If you notice your dogs persistently scratching his ears or shaking his head, he may have mites. In either case, make an appointment with the veterinarian immediately.
- Inspect teeth for tartar deposits. Some dogs accept weekly brushing with special brushes and canine toothpastes; in most cases, an adequate supply of dry, crunchy food minimizes deposits. Excessive buildup will have to be removed by a veterinarian, because the dog will have to be tranquilized.

Shorthairs

Short-haired dogs are relatively simple to groom. After thoroughly checking his body, use a fine-toothed comb and follow the lay of the fur. After combing, use a natural bristle brush, again following the lay of the fur. You can end the process by buffing his fur with a damp chamois cloth.

Longhairs

A little more effort is required to maintain the appearance of a long-haired dog. First, use a wire brush following the lay of the fur; then apply the brush against the lay. Again following the lay of the fur, apply a wide-toothed comb, starting at your dog's head and working down along his back; proceed down his sides and legs, and end with the ears and tail. Repeat this process, using a fine-toothed comb.

Dense Coats

Many dogs—particularly northern breeds such as Samoyeds, spitzes, and huskies—have dense undercoats, which contribute to the spectacular appearance of these breeds. During the winter months, the undercoat grows particularly thick, as a protection against the cold; even short-haired breeds tend to grow a slight undercoat during the winter. If you don't take steps to control shedding, you will go quite, quite mad once the weather turns warm.

An implement called a rake—which looks rather like a tiny saw with leather straps at each end—is typically used to loosen the undercoat each spring. Raking should be done outside, since the amount of hair extracted from an average Samoyed or Eskimo can probably fill a couple of laundry bags or a small futon. Grasping the leather straps, you curl the rake into a loop and draw it through the undercoat; avoid using excessive force, however, as no dog enjoys having its hair pulled out by the roots. If you're unfamiliar with the art of raking, you must consult a professional groomer before proceeding.

Wiry, Curly, or Unusual Coats

Poodles, terriers, spaniels, and unusual breeds such as the komondor or bichon frise require special attention. Their coats may need trimming, plucking, or cutting—delicate operations that require specially designed, sharp tools. Don't even attempt to perform any of these tasks without obtaining professional guidance and proper instruments. Some coats are not meant to be trimmed or plucked, and doing so will cause irreparable damage. In the best of all possible worlds, you should simply have a professional groomer handle these procedures once a month or so.

Nail Trimming

Overgrown nails can create any number of difficulties for a dog. They can become snagged in carpeting or furniture, for example, and in the course of trying to pry himself loose, your dog may rip off a toe. They can also curl backward into his paws, or prevent him from putting his feet down properly as he walks, ultimately leading to a painful sort of lameness. Dogs who do not spend much time outdoors are particularly likely to need a trim once a week or so, as their nails won't be worn down as quickly by outside activity.

If you introduce the procedure while your dog is young, he will usually submit gallantly later on in life. Older dogs who have never had their nails trimmed tend to greet the process with a fair amount of dread and fuss. Resistance presents a problem, especially for the novice pedicurist. A nerve and a vein run partly through each nail; if accidentally cut, the pain and bleeding can be intense. Some dogs have transparent nails, and the sensitive area appears as a reddish or purple streak. Many dogs, however, have dark or opaque nails, so trimming requires a fair degree of guesswork and precision.

If you have little or no experience trimming nails, or if your dog puts up a great deal of resistance, you're better off having a professional do the job. If, in time, your dog comes to accept the procedure, you can always ask your veterinarian or a groomer to show you how to perform the task yourself. Then again, you may just want to continue sending Max to the salon every month or so.

Bathing

Popular superstition holds that cats hate to be bathed, and dogs submit passively. Alas, most dogs do not enjoy soap and water any more than cats. Certain breeds with thick double coats, such as Old English sheepdogs or rough-haired collies, may only need bathing in extreme situations—for example, after rolling in mud or tangling with a skunk. Short-haired dogs may only need bathing when visitors begin to ask questions or hold their breath while talking. Adult dogs of any variety should not be bathed more than two or three times a year; puppies younger than six months should not be bathed at all, while dogs between the ages of six months and a year should only be bathed if necessary.

After a walk in the rain or splashing through mud, cleanup usually requires a quick rinse of legs and belly. You won't need soap, but you must be sure to dry wet areas thoroughly before allowing your dog to wander through the house or outdoors. Always rinse or bathe a dog indoors; if you wash him outside, he'll catch a chill, and probably get muddy. Stand your dog in a tub lined with a rubber mat to prevent slipping. Use lukewarm water, never hot or cold. If you are bathing your dog, use a shampoo recommended by your veterinarian; it should be gentle enough to protect your dog's skin and avoid causing tears.

After cleaning, pat your dog dry. Rubbing with a towel will produce mats or tangles, particularly in long coats. If you have a short-haired dog, keep him in a warm, draft-free room after patting him dry. Use a hand-held hair dryer and a brush to dry long-haired dogs; keep them away from drafts and don't let them outside for at least ten to twelve hours.

Dry baths provide a handy alternative to soap and water, especially if you need to clean a puppy who's tussled with a mud puddle. Simply work the powder into your dog's coat and brush it out. As with shampoos, ask your veterinarian to recommend an appropriate brand, and use only when required. Even dry-bathing your dog too frequently will eventually break down his coat.

BREEDING

Sooner or later, puppies grow up and begin to feel a certain restless urge. Males typically demonstrate their maturity by staining vertical surfaces with potently scented urine. At about the same time, they develop an uncanny ability to detect the scent of neighborhood females in heat, and will stop at nothing to satisfy the amorous compulsion that accompanies detection of said scent.

Females may enter into their first fertile cycle as early as six months old, although between eight and ten months seems to be more common. The fertile cycle is usually referred to as "heat," and among domestic dogs typically occurs twice a year. The first stage of the cycle, known as proestrus, is often marked by a thin, bloody discharge from the private parts. Proestrus generally lasts between five and twelve days, during which period Marcie is not fertile and will usually not tolerate sexual advances from over-excited males. She becomes fertile during the second stage, estrus, during which the discharge turns brown and somewhat more viscous. Estrus may last for seven to nine days, during which Marcie will relax her principles regarding males of her kind. At the end of this phase, if she has not found herself in the family way, her discharge will turn pale or milky, gradually diminishing in quantity until it disappears altogether.

The female cycle is not always obvious. Many dogs do not suffer distinct personality changes, and the discharge produced during all phases may be negligible. Because females become even more fastidious about bodily cleanliness while in heat, an unsuspecting owner may not be aware of the momentous changes taking place. Your only hint may be an impromptu gathering of romantic males around the front porch.

Before your dog reaches maturity, you should seriously contemplate the options available to you. If you own a pedigreed animal, you may wish to breed him or her. *Breeding involves more time and effort than you can possibly imagine.* Unless you have a good deal of experience, it is not recommended. The best solution is simply to have your dog neutered. Too many puppies enter this world unwanted, and are either abandoned or delivered to the gas chamber. You are ultimately responsible for whatever pain or suffering these innocents undergo. In a civilized world, you'd be hanged or beheaded for your negligence.

Pedigree Breeding

If you decide to breed your dog, you'll have to locate an appropriate partner for him or her; submit a number of affidavits confirming the dog's health; and work out a price for breeding service. If your dog is female, you'll have to provide medical care during pregnancy and after the pups are born. Before setting foot on the path, then, consider whether your dog is an outstanding example of its breed. It's essential not to pass on any hereditary problems or conditions. Consider well whether you can truly afford the time, money, and energy to see the project through to its completion. If you're absolutely determined to go ahead, consult your veterinarian before taking action.

Neutering

Some people object to the whole notion of interfering with a dog's reproductive integrity. Despite what may seem a generous or kindly motive, letting nature take her course can have a deleterious effect on dogs. Non-neutered males may develop aggressive habits, which can lead them to fight with other males; restless urges can meanwhile drive them to escape their homes and yards, and all too easily be struck by an automobile or carried off to the pound and destroyed. In the case of females, the hormonal stress of repetitive heat cycles may lead to complications such as ovarian cysts, urinary tract infections, and personality disorders. Nor is there a canine equivalent of menopause; females remain fertile for their whole lives.

Neutering is a fairly simple veterinary procedure. For males, it involves surgical removal of the testicles from the sac. Females undergo removal of the ovaries and all or part of the uterus, a procedure often referred to as "spaying." Both procedures require anesthesia, so you mustn't feed your dog the day before the operation. Following surgery, an overnight stay at the clinic or veterinarian's office is also required.

Males usually recover very quickly after neutering. You may have to make a few dietary adjustments, however, because a strictly or predominantly dry food diet can cause problems in the urinary tract. Since spaying is a more invasive procedure, females tend to heal more slowly; the recovery period typically lasts about a week. As with any surgical procedure, monitor your dog's behavior carefully. If swelling or infection develops, or your pet seems listless, has difficulty eliminating, or gnaws persistently at the stitches, contact your vet immediately.

The cost of neutering depends on the type of facility where the operation is performed. A number of adoption facilities offer low-cost or even free neutering, and local clinics may also offer a low rate. Private practice veterinarians usually charge a somewhat higher fee, though in return your pet will likely receive more attentive observation and aftercare. In addition, since spaying involves more complex surgery than castration, it is almost invariably more expensive.

An organization known as Friends of Animals may be able to direct you to a low-cost neutering facility in your area. They may also offer you reduced-rate certificates, which a private practice veterinarian in your area may accept. Friends of Animals may be reached at 1-800-321-7387.

HEALTH CARE

With dogs, as with people, there are no perfect models. Certain breeds are prone to genetic conditions, such as hip dysplasia or retinal deterioration. If you've researched your breed thoroughly, you'll know what to look for, and will discuss potential health problems with your veterinarian. More important, most dogs will spend a good deal of time outdoors—which means they'll come into contact with other dogs and a host of tiny or microscopic creatures that are no less committed to survival than you or your dog.

Naturally, you'll take your dog for an initial veterinary examination within a week of adoption. The veterinarian will examine coat, eyes, and ears; administer vaccinations, if necessary, and set up a booster schedule, and test for the presence of worms and other parasites. It would be nice to think you're home free after that, but your responsibility continues for the remainder of your dog's life. Accidents of various kinds can strike her and minor illnesses may lay her low for brief periods.

Home examinations, as described earlier in this chapter, can alert you to certain health problems. A basic familiarity with typical symptoms will help in this regard, and common diseases will be discussed later in this section. In addition to a basic daily examination, keep an eye out for other signs of illness. Symptoms include:

- General listlessness
- Difficulty walking
- Labored breathing
- Persistent coughing or vomiting
- Lack of coordination
- Failure to respond to sounds or movement
- Frequent or persistent soiling
- Inability to urinate, or painful urination

If your dog manifests any of these symptoms, contact your veterinarian immediately.

Battling the Elements

Depending on his age, coat, and breed, climatic extremes can adversely affect your dog. Puppies and small dogs—especially those with short coats—can easily become chilled during their daily walks. You will probably need to provide them with festive outerwear, available in most pet stores. While you don't need to go so far as to buy dog boots for your winter walks, you'll need to examine your dog thoroughly for salt, ice, and other chemicals as soon as you get inside.

Puppies, old dogs, longhairs, and certain flat-faced breeds like pugs and bulldogs are all prone to heat exhaustion in the summer months. You must be careful not to exercise them too hard when the weather turns warm; better yet, wait until evening. Always provide ample water after playtime or walking, and if you'll be spending long periods together out of doors, choose a shady spot where your dog can rest, and take along a bottle or a jug of water.

Vaccinations

Puppies who drink their mothers' milk within twenty-four hours of birth are typically protected against the diseases against which their mothers have been vaccinated. "First milk," or colostrum, contains a unique combination of proteins and antibodies that temporarily immunize a puppy for about twelve to sixteen weeks. Before this period ends, puppies must be vaccinated against various diseases. If the mother has not been vaccinated, or has low resistance to certain illnesses, her puppies may not be adequately protected.

Vaccination is essential to prevent occurrence of a variety of infectious diseases, including rabies, distemper, infectious canine hepatitis, canine leptospirosis, canine parvovirus, and two common respiratory infections, parainfluenza and bordetella, which can lead to a condition known as kennel cough. These will be discussed more thoroughly below. In order to develop immunities, puppies should receive initial vaccinations between six and eight weeks old, and are given boosters according to a schedule determined by your veterinarian. The following table represents a typical vaccination and booster schedule:

	6–8 weeks	10–12 weeks	12–16 weeks	14–16 weeks
Bordetella	✔	✔		✔
Parainfluenza	✔	✔		✔
Hepatitis	✔	✔		✔
Distemper	✔	✔		✔
Parvovirus	✔	✔		✔
Leptospirosis		✔		✔
Rabies			✔	

Most veterinarians recommend booster shots once a year, although a final parvovirus inoculation may be recommended at twenty weeks. Some states require administration of rabies boosters only once every three years. However, when planning to board or travel with your dog, always check the facility, state, or country's policy on rabies well in advance. If you've adopted an older puppy or dog, and do not have his medical records, don't automatically assume he's had his shots. Discuss the situation with your veterinarian when you bring your dog in for his first visit. Your vet will probably advise a complete vaccination series.

Young dogs and toys may experience a reaction to vaccines, which may involve a low-grade fever, muscle aches, sleepiness, or loss of appetite; such reactions typically last no longer than forty-eight hours. A very few dogs may suffer more pronounced symptoms, including hives, swelling of the face, or even vomiting. Again, the symptoms usually don't last more than two days, but it's wise to contact your vet in any case. Later, when it's time for a booster, remind the doctor of your pet's reaction. She may decide to administer an antihistamine. By no means should you skip a booster if your dog experiences a reaction.

Infectious Diseases

Vaccination, cleanliness, and daily examination are the best defense against disease. A basic knowledge of common canine diseases will not only help you appreciate the importance of vaccination but also alert you to symptoms should they arise. Your dog won't be able to tell you where something hurts or why, and if you ignore her problem for even a day or two in hopes that it will magically disappear, you may seriously jeopardize her life.

Respiratory Illness. Upper respiratory ailments are most often caused by adenovirus type II, parainfluenza virus, and bordetella. The first two are viral infections, which produce various flu-like symptoms such as coughing, sneezing, runny nose, and eyes, and difficulty breathing. Adenovirus type II is related to the virus that causes canine hepatitis, and vaccination against the latter will usually protect against the former. Bordetella is an extremely contagious bacterial infection. Bacteria is carried in saliva, mucus, and sputum, and quickly becomes airborne, infecting all dogs in the vicinity. The most obvious symptom is a dry, hacking, croup-like cough. These illnesses can occur singly or in combination, and can cause bronchitis and possibly pneumonia. Very young or old dogs, as well as those with allergies or flat faces, are particularly susceptible.

Infectious Canine Hepatitis. Unrelated to human hepatitis, the disease is caused by adenovirus type I, and spreads through contact with the body fluids of an infected dog. It produces an inflammation of the liver. The first symptom is usually a fever, followed by vomiting, appetite loss, abdominal pain, and swelling of the liver itself. Severe hepatitis infections can cause permanent liver damage. Other symptoms may or may not include jaundice, typified by a yellowing of the skin and body tissues, and a clouding of the cornea, commonly referred to as "blue eye." Blue eye may cause temporary or permanent blindness.

Distemper. This severe viral infection can be transmitted through contact with other dogs or through contact with someone or something that has come into contact with an infected dog. Initial symptoms include fever, conjunctivitis, sneezing, and coughing. Vomiting and diarrhea commence within a week or two of infection, often accompanied by weight loss and dehydration. Dogs who survive this stage of the disease suffer neurological disorders, including seizures, tremors, blindness, and difficulty walking. Treatment is limited, so only vaccination provides effective protection. For your dog's sake, always wash your hands after handling another dog, and don't let him play with another dog's toys.

Canine Parvovirus. Symptoms of this highly contagious intestinal virus are literally explosive: persistent, watery or bloody diarrhea, persistent vomiting, high fevers, and intense abdominal pain. The virus is usually spread through feces. Several strains are known, so you must consult your veterinarian for the most effective vaccine for your breed of dog.

Leptospirosis. A bacterial infection, leptospirosis principally attacks the liver, kidneys, and urinary tract. It is spread through the urine of infected dogs and rats, or small bodies of water contaminated thereby. Symptoms include fever, vomiting, depression, loss of appetite, and inflammation of the liver and/or kidneys, which can manifest as abdominal pain or back pain. Nosebleeds and eye infections may also occur. Severe infections may cause jaundice, abnormal movements, and foul breath. Leptospirosis can be communicated from dogs to people, though rarely the other way around.

Rabies. Rabies is a fatal disease, transmitted through the saliva or feces of an infected animal, such as a raccoon, bat, skunk, or fox. The incubation period can range from several days to more than a year before symptoms develop. The first symptoms include subtle behavioral changes, such as depression, mental dullness, or an urge for solitude, along with fever, slow eye reflexes, and chewing at the bite site. This stage, which may last two or three days, is followed by a two- to four-day period of erratic behavior, which may include irritability, pronounced aggression, snapping at inanimate objects or imaginary creatures, and extreme restlessness; disorientation and seizures may also occur. The final stage is characterized by paralysis at the bite site and of the face and jaw. Drooling, foaming, and a dropped jaw are not uncommon. Coma and death from respiratory paralysis follow shortly after the onset of the paralytic stage. There is no possibility of treatment once symptoms have developed.

If you suspect your dog has been bitten, he must be revaccinated and quarantined for at least ninety days. If he has not been vaccinated, he will have to be put to sleep. *Since rabies can be transmitted to humans, even when the infected animal shows no symptoms, it is imperative to protect yourself, and anyone with whom your dog comes into contact, through vaccination.*

Canine Coronavirus. This is another intestinal virus, though less violent in its effects than parvovirus. Symptoms include vomiting, diarrhea, and fever. Your vet may or may not vaccinate, depending on the incidence rate in your area.

Lyme Disease. Inoculation is controversial at this time; both the effectiveness and side effects of vaccinations are being reexamined. The best course, as always, is to consult your veterinarian. Symptoms of Lyme disease include fever, swelling or aching joints, loss of appetite, and lameness. The disease is transmitted by ticks, which leap from grass, brush, shrubbery, and other vegetation onto a warm-blooded host.

Tick prevention collars are available, although the best means of avoiding these parasites is to stay out of woods and grassy areas. Failing this, examine your dog thoroughly after a trek in the great outdoors. Since it usually takes twenty-four hours for the disease to pass from the tick to the host, prompt removal of the tick dramatically reduces the likelihood of infection. If your dog has been bitten by a tick, notify your veterinarian promptly.

Noninfectious Complaints

Noninfectious disorders may afflict your dog at some point during her life, regardless of your attention to her health. Some dogs are genetically prone to develop certain diseases. Others have little or no such genetic predisposition, and merely share the same unlucky fate of all living creatures. The following descriptions are offered simply as a precaution to alert you to potential health problems.

Allergies. Like people, dogs may suffer from a variety of allergic reactions. Topical allergies are most common, resulting from prolonged contact with wool, dust, newsprint, and cleansing materials; flea-related allergies are also familiar. Typical symptoms include skin inflammations or pigment changes. Some dogs experience allergic reactions to cigarette smoke, perfumes, and pollen, characterized by respiratory problems. Food allergies and allergic reaction to certain medications, such as antibiotics or anesthesia, usually result in nausea, vomiting, diarrhea, and appetite loss.

Eye-Related Disorders. Conjunctivitis typically produces a mucoid discharge, often accompanied by pronounced redness and tearing. Entropion, a condition that can affect certain breeds, occurs when one or both eyelids are turned inwards, causing itching, persistent blinking, and potential ulceration of the cornea. Ectropion is a condition in which one or both lids are turned outward, causing redness, tearing, and inflammation. Glaucoma results from a buildup of fluid pressure behind the eye, which can cause tearing, redness, dilated pupils, and sensitivity to light. Keratitis, an infection or ulceration of the cornea, often turns the cornea a bluish-white color; other symptoms include blinking, tearing, pain, and sensitivity to light. All eye-related disorders require prompt veterinary attention to prevent permanent damage to the eye.

Hip Dysplasia. Certain large breeds are genetically prone to a malformation of the hip joint, in which the socket and ball do not fit smoothly. Dysplasia can be diagnosed by X ray, and its effects minimized through proper nutrition and supplements. Untreated, it can lead to painful soreness and lameness.

Cystitis. Inflammation of the bladder, known as cystitis, can result from a bacterial infection. Over time, cystitis can cause painful urination, cloudy urine, or difficulty urinating. Severe infections can result in bladder stones or kidney stones, which can block the urethra entirely and completely prevent urination. This occurs primarily in male dogs. In such cases, toxins build up quite rapidly in the dog's system, causing vomiting and fever. Without immediate treatment, a dog will die. Aftercare often involves modifying the diet to reduce mineral content.

Kidney Disease. Infection of one or both kidneys inhibits a dog's ability to pass fluid toxins. He will typically compensate by attempting to drink more water, although persistent, and often severe, vomiting and diarrhea prevent him from retaining water. Treated promptly, an infection may not cause lasting damage to the kidneys. If not caught early enough, however, a chronic condition usually develops, which can only be partially controlled through medication and dietary modification.

Internal Parasites

Parasites are hardy, single-minded organisms that feed off the tissues of larger, living creatures. The internal variety primarily consists of various kinds of worms, though other creatures cause similar problems. They burrow inside a dog's digestive tract, causing unpleasant symptoms at best, and serious health problems at worst. Given half a chance, many will happily transport themselves from your dog's body to yours.

Probably the most common symptom of internal parasitic infestation is diarrhea, or loose, runny stools. If you suspect your dog has worms, notify your veterinarian, who will probably ask for a recent stool sample. Microscopic analysis is usually required to determine the identity of the parasite, which will, in turn, determine the type of medication used. Don't diagnose your dog yourself and employ an over-the-counter medication. Such medications may not prove effective against the type of worm your dog has, and most are highly toxic. More importantly, your dog may be suffering from some other type of infection.

The most common type of internal parasites follow.

Heartworm presents the most serious type of infestation. While other worms live in the intestines, heartworms attack the heart and blood vessels. They can grow from four to six inches long, and live inside your dog's heart for years. Treatment is difficult and not always successful. Heartworm is transmitted by mosquitoes, which suck the blood of an infected animal and inject developing larvae into their next victim. Infection may be minimized by limiting outdoor activities and keeping your dog in a screened area at night or on dark days. In areas where mosquito activity is intense, veterinarians may prescribe a drug to protect against heartworm infection—although you'll also need to have your dog screened every six months. Even in areas where there is little mosquito activity, you must have your dog screened for heartworm at least once a year.

Roundworms live in the intestines and feed off of digesting food. Symptoms include diarrhea, vomiting, anemia, potbellies, general lethargy. Puppies can die from a serious infestation. Larvae may also migrate into the tissues of children's skin. Since roundworm eggs are passed through an infested dog's stool, young children should be kept from areas where dogs have soiled. One need hardly stress the importance of cleaning up after your dog.

Hookworms may enter your dog's body either through the mouth or the skin. Because they live off blood sucked from the intestine walls, hookworms can cause severe anemia. Other symptoms include diarrhea (which may contain blood) and lethargy. Dirt, grass, dog runs, and kennels are likely areas where hookworm eggs and larvae lie in wait.

Tapeworms are usually transmitted through a secondary host, usually fleas, although rabbits, mice, and other domestic pets can be carriers. If your dog has fleas, or has suffered flea infestation, he may very well have tapeworms. The head of the worm attaches itself to the intestinal lining, while other parts, which contain eggs, break off and are passed through feces. These parts resemble small grains of white rice, and are easy to identify around the anus and in stool samples. The eggs are usually ingested along with the bodies of the secondary host. While you can't do much to keep your dog from swallowing fleas while he grooms himself, you can take steps to prevent them. You can also inhibit contact with other potential hosts, and make sure your other pets are free of tapeworms.

Whipworms and threadworms are less common. While the first type infests the large intestine, the latter lodges in the small. Both may cause diarrhea, anemia, and internal bleeding.

Giardia and *Coccidia* are not worms, but single-celled parasites that typically live in water contaminated by human or animal feces. Stream and river water are the most common sources of infection, so dogs should be discouraged from drinking them. However, since the municipal water supply of several major U.S. cities is also contaminated, you may wish to consider using a filter designed to eliminate these parasites—for your own health as well as your dog's.

External Parasites

These clever beasts embed themselves in a dog's coat or skin. Most forms are easy to manage, though given half a chance, they'll leap from Wolfgang's body to yours before you can say Miranda. If you wish to avoid embarrassing fits of scratching and twitching, deal with infestations as soon they develop.

The most common external parasites are:

Fleas are tiny brown, jumping creatures that burrow in your dog's fur and suck blood from his skin. They move faster than jack rabbits, and breed even more rapidly. A bath using special flea shampoo, followed by frequent powdering or spraying of the dog's body will usually kill fleas and eggs. Daily combing with a flea comb may serve as an additional—but not alternative— treatment. You will also have to annihilate refugees that have migrated to other parts of your home; fleas and flea eggs can live for more than a year in bedding, carpets, and cracks in the floor. You must treat your dog and your home simultaneously. Bombs, sprays or powders are usually effective, though potentially toxic. Less poisonous approaches are becoming more available, however; for the sake of your own and your dog's health, you should ask your veterinarian to recommend one of these methods.

Lice, like fleas, cause intense itching, but are somewhat easier to control using flea powders or sprays. Adult lice resemble small grains of rice; eggs look like dandruff.

Ticks fasten themselves to a dog's skin, particularly around the ears and toes. The surest way to remove these brutes is to pluck them off individually. First, dab each tick with rubbing alcohol to paralyze it; then use tweezers to pull it off, and drop it in a jar of alcohol. Don't use excessive force to remove the tick, as the head may remain embedded in your dog's skin. If it seems to resist, dab it with more alcohol. Afterward, wash all affected areas to prevent your dog from licking the alcohol. Ticks can transmit Lyme disease and several other debilitating, often fatal, diseases. These include Rocky Mountain spotted fever, a parasitic infection that causes a rash and severe flu-like symptoms; erlichiosis, a serious bacterial infection with flu-like symptoms; and babesiosis, an infectious disease of the blood system, the symptoms of which are sometimes mistaken for malaria. If your dog has been bitten by ticks, consult your veterinarian immediately. You should also be examined by your own doctor.

Mites of different varieties can cause itching and other uncomfortable symptoms. The most common type are ear mites, which produce a black discharge inside the ear; others live on the skin or burrow under it. All types are contagious, but may be destroyed through several applications of insecticide.

Communicable Diseases

Zoonoses, diseases that can be transmitted from animals to humans, constitute a serious hazard. For example, some worm infestations may cause problems for people. Perhaps the most serious threat comes from roundworms and hookworms. Roundworms are transmitted when canine feces, or soil contaminated by feces, is ingested. Babies and young children are probably most susceptible to accidental ingestion of this sort, but adults may just as likely forget to wash their hands after cleaning their dog or digging in the garden. Once roundworm larvae hatch in the digestive tract of a human host, they can migrate to the liver, the eyes, the kidneys, and even the brain.

Hookworms, by contrast, infest a human host through the skin. The most common example of transmission occurs while walking barefoot in a yard or field contaminated with canine feces; the worms actually burrow through the feet. Because a child's skin is often more supple than an adult's, children are most at risk. Hookworms remain under the skin, manifesting as extremely itchy, red eruptions.

Standard hygienic precautions can help offset the dangers of worm infestations. You must always clean up after your dog relieves himself, and wash your hands afterward. Dogs should not be allowed near sandboxes or other children's play areas, and young children especially should not be allowed near dog runs or other areas frequented by dogs. Shoes or sneakers must be worn in any outdoor area where a dog may have visited, and hands must be washed after any type of outdoor activity—whether work, pastime, or play.

Lice, fleas, and ticks, meanwhile, will happily leap from your dog to any person with whom he comes into contact. Lice and fleas cause painful itching and possible allergic reactions; ticks, moreover, can infect their human hosts with Lyme disease and

Rocky Mountain spotted fever. In addition, two of three types of mange mites common to dogs are transmissible to humans. Cheyletiella, or "walking dandruff," live off skin fluids. They cause severe, itchy dandruff on dogs, and itchy bites and crusty, yellow scabs on humans. Sarcoptic mange, known as scabies (or more commonly as crabs, due to their shape), burrow under the top layers of skin. Symptoms include intense itching and inflammation of the skin. Daily inspection of your dog's coat—especially after walking in a wooded area or field—will help to alert you to the possibility of infestation of external parasites. Any sign should be reported immediately to your veterinarian.

Finally, rabies, brucellosis, tetanus, and toxoplasmosis can be passed between dogs and humans. As discussed above, rabies is a viral infection, and is nearly always fatal among humans. It can be communicated through the saliva or feces of an infected dog. Brucellosis is a canine venereal disease, passed though semen or any sort of discharge from an infected female for several weeks after a birth or failed pregnancy. The disease can be absorbed through broken skin or mucus membranes. Like rabies, tetanus is active in canine saliva and can be communicated through dog bites. Toxoplasmosis, though more commonly present in feline feces than canine waste, is a single-cell parasite known to cause human birth defects.

In most cases, simple hygienic precautions will help to prevent infections. Children and adults alike should wash their hands after any outdoor activity, and after any contact with a dog. Dogs should be isolated from children's play areas, and toys, gardening implements, and other objects left outside should be sprayed or washed before handling. Any dog bite must be cleaned immediately and receive immediate medical attention. Pregnant women should stay away from gardens, sandboxes, and other areas where dogs may have relieved themselves, and should never handle canine waste.

Administering Medication

As part of treatment, a veterinarian may prescribe certain medications to be given once or several times daily. Some dogs patiently allow you to give them foul-tasting drops or pills; others make a scene. Attempts to disguise medication in dog food or a special treat may succeed, but some dogs are clever enough to see through the ruse.

The easiest way to administer a pill sounds more complicated in theory than in practice. Hold the pill between the thumb and index finger of one hand, using the remaining fingers to press down on your dog's lower jaw. Place the thumb of your other hand just behind the large upper fang and gently press upward to tilt your dog's head back. Drop the pill deep into his mouth, remove your fingers, and hold his jaw firmly shut while you gently rub his throat to engage his swallowing reflex. Afterward, tap him lightly on the nose. If he licks it, he's swallowed the pill.

Administering liquid medication sounds easier, but tends to be a bit messy if your dog is at all reluctant. It helps to put a single dose of the medication into a small, squeezable bottle; don't use a stoppered glass tube, as your dog may inadvertently bite down and swallow fragments of glass. Gently insert the index and middle fingers of one hand into the corner of his mouth and pull down on the lower lip to form a sort of pocket; use your thumb to tilt his head very slightly upward. Holding the bottle in your other hand, pour a few drops of the liquid into the pocket, adding more as your dog swallows.

If your dog doesn't like to have his mouth touched, or has a tendency to bite, you'll have to ask your veterinarian how best to administer liquid and solid medication. Intravenous or subcutaneous injections—which may be necessary for certain illnesses such as diabetes or kidney conditions—absolutely require detailed instruction by a veterinarian. Never give your dog a shot without proper instruction, as you may injure her or yourself, and very likely deposit the medication in the wrong area.

Emergency Care

In case of accident, injury, or other emergency, you may need to take immediate steps to handle the situation until you can bring your dog to a hospital or veterinarian's office. Injured dogs are often frightened, and even the sweetest animal may prove uncooperative or aggressive. Still, timely action may mean the difference between life and death. You may be able to control any tendency to snap or bite by wrapping a towel or a long piece of gauze around the dog's muzzle. Be very careful not to cover the dog's nostrils, however, as she may suffocate.

As a precaution, it's a good idea to keep a first-aid kit in a convenient, easy-to-find location. The kit should include:

- Scissors
- Tape
- Bandages
- String or rope
- A blanket or thick towel, to be used for restraint or cases of severe bleeding or shock
- Hydrogen peroxide (to induce vomiting)
- Kaopectate or Pepto-Bismol™
- Antibiotic ointments (for eyes and skin)
- A flat board, to be used as a stretcher, if necessary

Also, make sure you know the location and telephone number of the nearest animal hospital or clinic that offers twenty-four-hour emergency service. The address and phone number should be clearly written out in the same location as your veterinarian's number.

The most likely emergency situations you may face include:

Heat Exhaustion and Heatstroke. Hard exercise in the summer months can cause heat exhaustion, especially among young or old dogs, longhairs, and dogs with flat faces. Any dog may succumb if left inside a parked car. Signs of heat exhaustion include excessive panting, labored breathing, and flushing or redness inside the ear. Heat exhaustion can swiftly degenerate into heatstroke, which is often signaled by weakness, dizziness, difficulty walking, and/or loss of consciousness. Only prompt action can save your dog's life. At the onset of symptoms, cool him down as quickly as possible; hose him with cool water, or apply an ice pack or ice wrapped in a towel or blanket to his head. Then waste no time transporting him to an animal hospital.

Bleeding. Cuts or gashes may cause profuse bleeding, which may be controlled by the application of a pressure bandage. If nothing of the sort is available, wrap a clean sock or towel over the wound, or layer the area with paper towels; then wrap an adhesive bandage or a length of rope or string around the makeshift padding. If the bleeding is severe, wrap the dog in a towel before transporting her to the vet or clinic; this will help to prevent shock, and absorb blood.

Embedded Objects. Hooks, thorns, needles, pins, and other sharp objects may become embedded in your dog's paws or mouth. Do not attempt to remove these objects; in almost all cases, the animal must be sedated or anesthetized. Confine or contain your dog, and call your vet or local animal hospital at once.

Fractures and Shock. If your dog falls from a very high place, is hit by a moving vehicle, or gets caught by a slamming door, he may suffer broken bones and will probably go into shock. In particular, broken legs must be immobilized promptly to minimize damage that might occur to blood vessels, nerves, and tendons. Wrap a towel, several washcloths, or several layers of newspaper or paper towel around the fracture and fix the layers in place with tape, string, or rope. Wrap the animal in towels or blankets to conserve body heat and transport him to a hospital or emergency facility. Take another person along, if at all possible, to keep the injured dog physically stable during the ride to the hospital.

Swallowed Objects. Something small enough to swallow may very likely pass through the dog's body without causing harm. However, sharp objects, such as needles, tacks, pins, or earring backs, may puncture the lining of the digestive tract. To cushion the object along the way, feed your dog small bits of bread soaked in milk, and contact your veterinarian as soon as possible to discuss further steps.

Poisoning. Dogs can easily become poisoned through grooming fur that has come into contact with a toxic substance. Plant nibbling and accidental ingestion of human medications are also common causes. If your dog has come into contact with a toxic substance such as cleaning solutions, paint, tar, or antifreeze, wash it off with soap and warm water before he has a chance to lick it off. If necessary, give him a complete bath in lukewarm (not cold) water.

If you don't catch your dog in time, you may need to induce vomiting. For medium or large dogs, give one teaspoon of hydrogen peroxide (3 percent solution) every ten minutes for half an hour; for small dogs, give no more than a quarter teaspoon. To prevent absorption of any chemical or toxin that remains, your vet may advise you to administer Kaopectate, Pepto-Bismol, or oral charcoal capsules, so it's wise to keep these on hand. Don't attempt to induce vomiting if your dog has swallowed an acid, alkali, solvent, heavy-duty cleaner, petroleum product, medication, or any type of sharp object; shows symptoms of lethargy or appears comatose; or has swallowed the substance more than two hours prior to the onset of symptoms. You may attempt to coat the digestive tract with milk, egg whites, or vegetable oil; however, it is essential to check the label of any toxic substance to make sure these things will not react adversely. In all cases of poisoning, bring your dog to an emergency clinic or hospital as soon as possible.

Gastric Torsion or "Bloat." Large dogs are prime candidates for this extremely serious condition, which can occur if the dog is induced to play or exercise too soon after gobbling down a large quantity of food. Symptoms include restlessness, discomfort, stomach pain, distended abdomen, nausea, gagging, persistent swallowing, and labored breathing. Often, afflicted dogs will not want to lie down; rather than a sign of improvement, such refusal signals imminent death. If not treated within two hours of the onset of symptoms, the condition is invariably fatal. Therefore, if you even suspect gastric torsion, contact your veterinarian immediately.

Transporting Ill or Injured Dogs

If your dog is small, hold him by the skin of the neck and the rump and slide him gently onto a blanket or into a box with its side folded down. Avoid all unnecessary movements that may shift his backbone, legs, or tail. Once you have transferred the animal to a box, wrap him in blankets to keep him warm and minimize shifting; then transfer the box to your car. Large dogs may be slid gently onto a blanket or a blanket-lined board and carefully dragged or carried to the car. More than one person will be needed to lift a large dog into a car without damaging his back and legs.

Obviously, this procedure is easier to accomplish if the dog is unconscious or dazed. If he's conscious, keep talking to him every step of the way, as the sound of your voice will reassure him. If he puts up a fight, his condition is probably not too serious. Let him lie or sit comfortably in the car with you while you transport him to the veterinarian's office or the nearest clinic. Drive cautiously to avoid upsetting him; otherwise he may try to bite you or move around. If at all possible, have someone accompany you, to soothe the animal and make sure he remains as still as possible.

IN SUM

Altogether, the material presented in this chapter may paint a rather dire picture of canine care. To be sure, accepting responsibility for a living creature—particularly a lively, clever, curious one such as a dog—is no light matter. Far better to understand all the potential hazards and pitfalls of ownership at once than to let ignorance sow the seeds of tragedy. Regular visits to the veterinarian can help to keep your pet in the bloom of health for many years to come. And so long as you exercise common sense and take proper precautions both in and outside your home, life with a dog can be simple, pleasant, and enormously rewarding.

Chapter 7

Last Words

Dogs age at different rates, depending on their size. Giant breeds grow old faster, typically departing this world at about eight or nine years old. Small dogs, on the other hand, age much more slowly. A poodle or terrier can live for twelve to fifteen years, while certain toy breeds may enjoy the pleasures of earthly life even longer. Individual characteristics and circumstances play a role in the drama of aging. So the figures mentioned above must be considered statistical probabilities, rather than reliable predictions.

The first year of a dog's life is roughly equivalent to fourteen years in human terms. By the end of her second year, a dog is already a young adult of twenty-four. Thereafter, each year of life measures between six and seven years of human life. Thus, in human terms, a nine-year-old dog is about sixty-three years old. After ten years, the ratio diminishes somewhat, with one year of a dog's life equivalent to four years of a person's. By fifteen years, each canine year roughly equals two human years; so a twenty-year-old Pekingese can be said to have reached the ripe old age of ninety-five.

In the case of large breeds, body metabolism begins to slow after five years. For smaller breeds, the changes will occur more slowly, over a longer period. You may notice slight personality changes, typically associated with the passage of youthful vigor. Felicity may seem less lively or more attached to her routine; she may even develop midriff bulge. At this point, diet and exercise become no less important for a dog than for a person. No doubt, the modern trend toward specialization will eventually produce canine exercise gurus and diet consultants. Until then, however, you and your veterinarian must devise a program that will keep your dog trim.

As your dog enters her golden years, she will likely show further signs of age. She may not be able to walk as far, or as long, as she was once able to do. Instead of leaping up on you as you come in the door, she may simply raise her graying muzzle and blink her wise old eyes. At this point, semiannual veterinary exams will help to detect any latent health problems as early as possible, and minimize the discomfort associated with them. A number of holistically oriented veterinarians have developed specialized programs for maintaining the health of older dogs.

SPECIAL NEEDS OF OLDER DOGS

As your dog paces slowly toward the other shore, physical changes become more apparent. The gradual decline of her thyroid, adrenal glands, pancreas, and kidneys may result in chronic renal failure, hypothyroidism, or diabetes. She may become more susceptible to respiratory diseases, and more sensitive to changes in temperature. Outward signs of age include:

- Cloudy eyes
- Thinning coat
- Prominent bones
- Loose skin
- Stiff joints and muscles
- Weakened senses
- Susceptibility to illness

She may become cranky and less tolerant of changes in her environment. She may nod off after dinner, or pad around the house complaining half the night.

Diet

Old dogs often lose their sense of smell. Any impairment will very likely affect their appetite, since aroma tempts them toward the breakfast bowl much more powerfully than the taste of dog food. You may need to offer more robustly scented meals as an encouragement to eat. Whatever brand you buy should meet the requirements of the Association of American Feed Control Officials (AAFCO). The label should state this clearly. Depending on your dog's needs, your veterinarian may also recommend vitamin and mineral supplements.

At the same time, progressive weight loss can also indicate renal failure, liver disease, cancer, or other types of illnesses. It's therefore imperative to keep an accurate weekly or monthly record of your dog's weight; if you notice any significant changes or sudden dips, notify your veterinarian. Should your dog develop a constant thirst and urinate more frequently than before, she may have developed diabetes; alternatively, her poor old kidneys may be having a harder time processing toxins, in which case your vet may prescribe a low-protein diet.

Exercise

With age, dogs are less inclined toward exercise. If arthritis sets in, unexercised muscles will lose their strength and elasticity, and circulation will suffer. Massage can stimulate blood flow, while relieving soreness and improving muscle tone. Regular activity is also necessary, albeit on a much more limited scale than earlier observed. Bear in mind, too, that your dog may now need more frequent trips outside to relieve herself, since her bladder is no longer elastic enough to hold urine for ten or twelve hours at a time. She may, on occasion, have an accident indoors.

Skin and Coat

As your dog ages, her skin will grow less soft and supple. Flaking and itching are not uncommon, and a dry, listless coat may develop as a result. Your dog may also be subject to rashes or other skin problems. Ask your vet about special shampoos that can help to maintain the skin's moisture balance. Adding oil or vitamin supplements to the diet may also prove beneficial, if your veterinarian advises. Promptly report any lumps or lesions you discover during daily grooming.

Eyes

You may notice cloudiness or discharge. If the condition persists, consult your veterinarian. Your dog's eyes may become filmy or gray, which may or may not indicate cataracts. If cataracts develop, your dog may go blind. This is not the worst tragedy that can befall an aging dog. So long as you maintain a close watch over her inside and outside the house, maintain her daily routine of eating and exercise, and don't drastically disarrange her envi-

The classic bestseller that began James Herriot's extraordinary series...

All Creatures Great and Small

JAMES HERRIOT

Let the world's most beloved animal doctor take you along on his wonderful adventures through the Yorkshire dales as he tends to its unforgettable inhabitants—four-legged and otherwise.

"This warm, joyous and often hilarious first-person chronicle of a young animal doctor...shines with love of life."

—*The New York Times Book Review*

ronment, she will be able to get around fairly well; do not let her go up or down stairs on her own, however. While outside, take care to protect her against other dogs and moving vehicles, and if possible, don't deviate from the route she was used to walking.

Age-Related Illness

Your dog may sail smoothly into her final years. She is just as likely, however, to suffer many of the same afflictions that affect people as they age. As her immune system weakens, she may become more susceptible to disease; coughs and colds are not uncommon, and infections may take longer to heal. More severe problems, meanwhile, can arise from the degeneration of the internal organs. Among the more common complaints of aging are:

Cancer. The possibility of developing tumors or lesions increases with age. Females that have never been spayed, or spayed late in life, are especially likely to develop breast cancer. Chemotherapy or surgery may alleviate some of the discomfort associated with the disease, but rarely lead to complete remission.

Heart Disease. Symptoms of heart disease include coughing, lethargy, loss of appetite, and sleepiness. Since these are also normal signs of old age, they may easily be overlooked until the heart and circulation have degenerated beyond repair. Keep an eye out for more specific symptoms, such as panting, labored breathing, breathing with an open mouth, occasional paralysis of the back legs, and a bluish cast to the tongue.

Liver Disease. Like any organ, the liver may degenerate with advancing age. Symptoms of liver malfunction include jaundice, vomiting, poor appetite, listlessness, difficulty walking, and dizziness. While liver disease is nearly impossible to cure, medications and dietary management as prescribed by a veterinarian can help reduce the signs of disease.

Renal Failure. The most common signs of kidney disease are weight loss, loss of appetite, bad breath, increased thirst, frequent urination, and occasional vomiting. Symptoms are caused by an accumulation of toxic wastes. Medication and a reduced-protein diet can sometimes minimize the effects of toxic accretion. Specially formulated foods can usually be prescribed by a veterinarian.

Diabetes. Excessive thirst, voracious appetite, and heavy urination may point to an insulin imbalance. The problem can be controlled by a change of diet and daily medication.

DEATH

Death may come suddenly, without any sign of distress or illness; occasionally, too, symptoms manifest only after a disease has entered its final stages. An abrupt end is often far more difficult to fathom than a gradual decline. It's difficult to prepare for the loss of a dog, in any case, no matter how one resents the daily responsibilities of ownership. The leash hangs idly by the door; at the appointed time, no happy bark sounds in anticipation of a walk in the rain. Where once was life, duty, comfort, a teeth-gritting juggling of schedules, there is only absence—less than nothing.

When your dog appears unresponsive to touch, when she suddenly becomes limp or seems to stare, not at you, but through you, her time is near. If she's in pain, unable to breathe normally, or unlikely to resume normal functioning, the kindest course is to allow your veterinarian to assist her to a quiet, painless end. It is not an easy decision to make, but one must temper hope of miraculous recovery with concern that your dear friend no longer suffer in this world.

The veterinarian may first administer a sedative, such as Valium, to calm your dog if she's agitated. Afterward, a large dose of pain medication will swiftly, gently carry her away. Hearing is the last sense to fade, so as she leaves, by all means continue to stroke her and talk to her. It will be a comfort in the days to come if you know that her last experience on this earth is your voice, letting her know how much you love her, and how much her company has meant.

Appendices

Appendix A: Registries and Publications

Registries:

The American Kennel Club
51 Madison Avenue
New York, NY 10010
(212) 696-8200
http://www.akc.org

The United Kennel Club
100 East Kilgore Road
Kalamazoo, MI 49001
(616) 343-9020
http://www.ptialaska.net/~pkalbaug/ukcindex.html

Publications:

The AKC Gazette
51 Madison Avenue
New York, NY 10010
Subscriptions: (919) 233-9780

Bloodlines
100 East Kilgore Road
Kalamazoo, MI 49001
(616) 343-9020

Canine Health Naturally
P.O. Box 69, Dept C
Lions Bay, B.C., Canada V0N 2E0
Phone/Fax: (604) 921-7784

Wolf Clan Magazine
3952 N. Southport Ave., Suite 122, Dept C
Chicago, IL 60613

Appendix B: Pet Insurance

Your veterinarian or your local animal shelter or hospital may be able to discuss insurance plans that help to defray the costs of emergency and major medical care. Benefits vary according to each plan, and may be limited to member veterinarians or clinics. Basic plans typically cost about one hundred dollars per year, in exchange for percentage reductions in costs. Limits may apply, and you will probably have to pay for certain exclusions and deductibles.

If your veterinarian or clinic cannot advise you, you may choose to contact one of the following organizations for more information:

RLI Planned Services Inc.
Dept. CF9025 N. Lindbergh Drive
Peoria, IL 61615

Pet Assure Inc.
Sales Department
15 Penn Plaza. OF-2
New York, NY 10001
1-888-789-PETS

Anipals, Inc.
899 S. College Mall Rd. #242
Bloomington, IN 47401
1-888-ANIPALS

Appendix: C: Toxins

Food. Anything rotten, moldy, or suspiciously aged; bones; caffeine; chocolate; nuts; onions; pork; raw meat; raw potatoes.

Medications. Acetaminophen (Tylenol); antihistamines; aspirin (except as directed by a veterinarian); benzocaine (topical anaesthetic); benzyl alcohol; diet pills; heart preparations; hexachlorophene (found in medicated soaps, such as pHiso-Hex); ibuprofen; methylene blue; methyl salicylate; phenazopyridine; phenytoin (Dilantin); phosphate enemas; sleeping pills; tranquilizers; vitamins; anything smelling of wintergreen.

Chemical substances:

Rat/roach poisons: Phosphorus (also found in fireworks, matches, matchboxes, and fertilizers); sodium fluoroacetate; strychnine; warfarin (also prescribed in anticoagulants for people); zinc phosphide.

Slug/snail bait, ant traps, weed killers, and insecticides: Arsenic; metaldehyde.

Household cleaning agents: Bleach; carbamates; chlorinated hydrocarbons; corrosives (e.g., household cleaners, drain openers, solvents); metal polish; fungicides; furniture polish; phenol; phosphates; pine oil.

Other common household chemicals and toxic items: Antifreeze; brake fluid; dye; hair products; lead (found in commercial paints, linoleum, and batteries); matches; mothballs; petroleum products (e.g., gasoline, kerosene, turpentine); photographic developer solutions; shoe polish; soaps; suntan lotions; windshield fluid; wood stains.

Plants:

Topical allergic reactions: Chrysanthemum; creeping fig; poinsettia; pot mum; spider mum; weeping fig.

Fatal swelling of the mouth, tongue and/or throat: Arrowhead vine; Boston ivy; caladium; dumbcane; emerald duke; majesty; marble queen; nephthytis; parlor ivy; pathos; philodendron; red princess.

Produces vomiting and diarrhea: Bittersweet woody; castor bean; daffodil; delphinium; foxglove; ground cherry; Indian turnip; Indian tobacco; larkspur; poke weed; skunk cabbage; soapberry; wisteria.

Can cause vomiting, abdominal pain, cramps, tremors, as well as heart, respiratory and/or kidney problems: Amaryllis; angel's trumpet; asparagus fern; azalea; bird of paradise; buttercup; creeping Charlie; crown of thorns; dologeton; Dutchman's breeches; elephant ears; glocal ivy; heart ivy; jasmine; Jerusalem cherry; jimsonweed; locoweed; lupine; matrimony vine; May apple; mescal bean; moonseed; mushrooms; needlepoint ivy; nightshade; pigweed; poison hemlock; pot mum; rhubarb; ripple ivy; spider mum; spinach; sprangeri fern; sunburned potatoes; tomato vine; umbrella plant; water hemlock.

Toxic shrubbery and trees: Almond; American yew; apricot; balsam pear; black locust; cherry; English holly; English yew; horse chestnut/buckeye; Japanese plum; mock orange; peach; privet; rain tree/monkey pod; Western yew; wild cherry.

Greenhouse plants: Many plants purchased from a commercial greenhouse have been sprayed with chemical pesticides. Always ask what sprays have been used, how long the spray lasts, and whether or not the leaves and stems can be cleaned; you may also request material safety data for all chemicals used.

Poisonous Animals. Bufo toads. (Found in various areas, especially in southern Florida; if ingested, can kill a small dog in a matter of minutes.)